Handwriting Analysis

Handwriting Analysis

BY CHRIS MORGAN

SMITHMARK

A QUINTET BOOK

First published in the United States
by SMITHMARK Publishers Inc.
16 East 32nd Street, New York, NY 10016.

SMITHMARK books are available for bulk
purchase for sales promotion and premium use.
For details write or telephone
the Manager of Special Sales
SMITHMARK Publishers Inc.
16 East 32nd Street, New York, NY 10016
(212) 532-6600.

ISBN 0-8317-4205-4

This book was designed and produced by
Quintet Publishing Limited
6 Blundell Street
London N7 9BH

Creative Director: Richard Dewing
Designer: Chris Dymond
Project Editor: Damian Thompson
Editor: Joy Wotton
Picture Researcher: Jill de Cet
Photographer: Mirco de Cet

Typeset in Great Britain by
Central Southern Typesetters, Eastbourne
Manufactured by
Bright Arts (Singapore) Pte Ltd
Printed in Singapore by
Star Standard Industries Private Ltd

Contents

Introduction

Your handwriting shows what sort of a person you are.

Introvert or extrovert, clear or muddled thinker, leader or follower, sensual or frigid, slap-dash or precise, modest or boastful, aggressive or conciliatory – whichever you are, it is all laid out in your handwriting. The skilled graphologist (analyst of handwriting) will be able to interpret your personality with great accuracy from a page of your writing. Even without skill and experience, it is possible to use a book such as this to interpret the characters of your family, friends and colleagues.

Your handwriting is probably unique. Because of the many factors involved in a style of writing, it is most unlikely that any two people would write identically, just as it is most unlikely that two people will have the same fingerprints.

And, just as with fingerprints, there are key factors that cannot be learnt from a handwriting sample. One is a person's age. Although an experienced graphologist might be able to make an informed guess about age from circumstantial evidence, there is no accurate means of telling age from handwriting. Another factor is sex. No absolute distinguishing marks exist to enable men's and women's handwriting to be separated. Nor can left- or right-handedness be established. Although there is a tendency for the writing of left-handers to lean very slightly more to the left (due to posture rather than personality), there is no other consistent difference between the groups. Nationality and race, too, are impossible to distinguish from handwriting.

Neither can the analysis of handwriting be used to predict the writer's future, despite some claims to the contrary.

So what are the uses of graphology? Apart from the obvious entertainment value of interpreting the character defects of yourself and those around you, there are several important practical applications. Graphology can be a valuable aid to personnel selection and vocational guidance (some organizations have employed it as part of their selection procedure for the last fifty years). It is used in criminal detection, particularly in the verification of signatures in fraud and forgery cases. It can be a good, scientific means of selecting a prospective marriage partner (though it is most unusual for anyone to pick their husband or wife scientifically). And it is a valuable tool in the diagnosis of mental and physical illness.

A warning before you start the book: most people's writing contains some contradictory signs, so try not to make any character pronouncement on the basis of only one or two factors.

Chris Morgan
January 1992

Graphology is used extensively in forensic investigations of crime. When the son of aviator Charles Lindbergh (pictured) was kidnapped in 1927, handwriting analysts helped to clinch the case against Bruno Hauptmann. Samples of his handwriting were found to match the ransom note.

7

CHARACTER CASE STUDY: Winston Churchill

LETTER WRITTEN TO KING GEORGE VI IN 1915

Ink-filled loops and ovals
These show sensuality and a tendency to self-indulgence.

Garland connections
These indicate friendliness and affection.

Angles and positive downstrokes
These indicate toughness and determination.

Upstrokes on the "p"
These denote an enterprising and prudent character.

Connectedness and speed
The fluidity and cohesiveness of the writing – its evenness – show an ability to co-ordinate and progress his thoughts and actions spontaneously. The extended "t" bar emphasizes his protectiveness toward people and events.

Figure-8 "g"s
These show an awareness of time passing as well as a firm resolve.

Small middle zone
This indicates a confident and discreet personality with good strategic skills.

Greek "d"s and "e"s
These illustrate a cultured and aesthetic mind and/or background.

Enlarged and "thready" signature
The signature written in a larger hand shows that he was well aware of his identity and importance; the threadiness indicates his diplomatic skills and also that the content of the letter is more important than the identity of the writer.

Analysis of Churchill's Character

This is the writing of a well-coordinated, enterprising, determined and quick mind – undoubtedly a man who ferrets out information and uses it to his best advantage. He has the ability to plan ahead carefully. Whilst he has the odd flight of fancy and is willing to take calculated risks, he leaves very little to chance.

Determined, even pigheaded, at times, he will plough doggedly on against all the odds. Unafraid of opposition and controversy, he in fact works best when under pressure. He will follow his gut reaction when all else fails. Should he find himself in a tight corner, he has both the wit and charm to wriggle his way out of the compromising situation.

An articulate and erudite man, he enjoys being "centre stage" and orchestrating the lives of others. He does not suffer fools gladly and will abruptly break off relationships which do not meet his high expectations. Very concerned with the passage of time, he has learned the importance of knowing when to move forward and when to hold back, although periods of inactivity frustrate him, and he will absorb himself in physical labours to exhaust his considerable nervous energy.

The rigidity and toughness he displays when following through a programme of work, together with his singularity of purpose, make him a formidable competitor in any venture.

Basically a friendly man who beneath a rather brusque and impatient exterior has a kindly and romantic attachment toward his close family and friends – he is also deeply dependent upon their support, something he finds very hard to admit. His tremendous degree of protectiveness toward his beliefs, ideals and ambitions can be misconstrued as self-absorption and a desire to dominate everyone and everything around him.

A very sensuous and tactile man. He would drink in not only the scent and colour of a rose, but also feel its texture and form. A sculpture is not something just to be looked at; it must be handled to experience its true beauty.

His rich imagination, eye for detail, excellent memory and innate curiosity all show him to be an avid reader. They are traits which also enhance his ability to express himself most eloquently.

How the Analysis Was Made

● Measurement of the handwriting with ruler and protractor shows it to be almost equal in proportion throughout the upper and lower zones. There is also a classic degree of rightward slant. This indicates that the head and the heart have equality in his character and reasoning.

● The middle zone is the least prominent and the smallness of letter size here indicates that this man is confident and uses discretion and strategy to obtain his most important desires.

● The extended upward strokes on the letter "p" confirm this man's determination and his ability to be diligent and enterprising.

● Greek "e"s and "d"s confirm his aesthetic and artistic ability, as do the ink-filled ovals and loops. They also indicate that he enjoys the "good things" in life, which act as "comforters".

● Spacing of the words and lines is clear, emphasizing his need for his own time and space; however, in some sections of the passage of writing the words, although clearly defined, are quite close to each other, stressing his reliance upon the support of those he loves and trusts.

● The letters "s" and "g" in the form of the figure 8 illustrate his awareness of the importance of the passage of time. These, as well as the positive downstrokes, confirm his toughness of mind and will to succeed.

A brief history of handwriting analysis

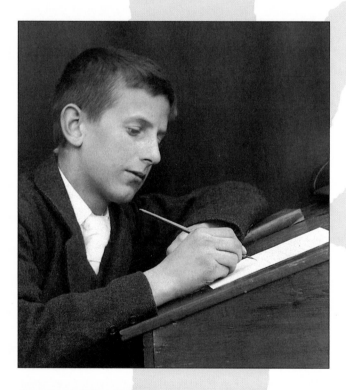

A schoolboy at work with a quill pen in around 1900. He would have been taught rigorously to follow either Copperplate or its variant, the Vere Foster.

Despite occasional much earlier references to handwriting and its meaning, the first books on graphology appeared in the 17th century. *Ideographica* by Alderius Prosper was published in Bologna early in the century. Then, in 1622, Camillo Baldo of Baldi, an Italian physician, wrote a book in Greek whose title translates as *An Essay on the Means of Examining the Character and Qualities of a Writer from his Letters*. Both books were fairly obscure and were generally ignored.

A century later there was some small interest in the subject in France, but this achieved little, and it was not until about 1830 that handwriting began to be studied seriously and continuously. This was done by some French clerics, of whom Abbé Flandrin (1806–81) was the most important. Flandrin's student, Abbé Jean Hippolyte Michon, who coined the term graphology in 1871, proved to be the father of the subject and wrote famous early textbooks on it. With his pupil, Jules Crépieux Jamin, he created the so-called school of isolated signs. They related specific handwriting aspects to traits of character, though without attempting to explain their psychological significance. Later, Jamin worked with Alfred Binet in the further development of graphology. These were the experimenters who made France the home of graphology during the 19th century.

Handwriting in different cultures

Although handwriting has existed for some 5,500 years, since the time of the ancient Sumerians, for very nearly all that time it was a specialized art or skill, practised by only a few. Originally all writers were members of priesthoods. Only gradually did the knowledge spread to members of the ruling classes, to specialist scribes, to professional people (doctors, scientists) and then to merchants and other members of the middle class. Even in the US, Britain and continental Europe, most people went through their lives being unable to write (or to read) until the 19th century, when working-class children began to attend school in large numbers.

Children in 19th-century Britain were taught Copperplate writing, which was generally in use when government schools' inspectors began their inspections in 1839 and was incorporated into school curriculums officially from 1870. Simpler versions of Copperplate were introduced in later decades, including the Vere Foster method and Civil Service script.

Another experiment, in some schools, was Print script (also known as Running script), which was introduced in the 1920s and was a very simple "ball and stick" style with letters that were not joined up. From the mid-1930s, the Marion Richardson style was also taught in schools; its rounder, simpler and more upright form was intended to be easier for children to learn but more characterful than Print script. Despite some different learning scripts developed since then, the Marion Richardson style is still taught. At the same time, some schools in Britain and in continental Europe have taught (and are still teaching) Italic script.

In the US many different scripts have been taught, though nearly all are more ornate and right slanted than the Marion Richardson style and some are more so than Copperplate. The best known, still widely in use, is the Palmer method, very looped and cursive.

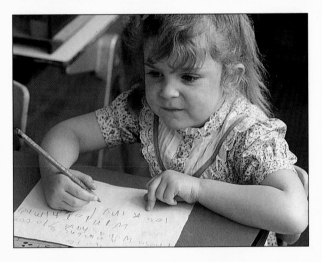

Clarity is the touchstone in today's taught handwriting styles. Children learn the Marion Richardson method in British schools, while the more ornate Palmer script is employed in the US.

Official styles

𝒜 𝐵 𝒞 𝒟 𝒠 𝒡 𝒢 𝒣 𝒦 𝒧 𝒨 𝒩
𝒪 𝒫 𝒬 𝒭 𝒮 𝒯 𝒰 𝓋 𝒲 𝒳 𝒴 𝒵
𝒶 𝒷 𝒸 𝒹 𝒺 𝒻 𝒼 𝒽 𝒾 𝒿 𝓀 𝓁 𝓂 𝓃 𝑜 𝓅
𝓆 𝓇 𝓈 𝓉 𝓊 𝓋 𝓌 𝓍 𝓎 𝓏 & &c &c

Thomas E. Hill – USA, 1870s

ABCDEFGHIJKLMNOPQRSTUVWXYZ
abcdefghijklmnopqrstuvwxyz

Vere Foster – British, 1898

ABCDEFGHIJKLMNOPQRSTUVWXYZ
abcdefghijklmnopqrstuvwxyz

Palmer script – USA, 1980s

ABCDEFGHIJKLMNOPQRSTU VWXYZ
abcdefghijklmnopqrstuvwxyz

Marion Richardson – British, 1935 to date

ABCDEFGHIJKLMNOPQR STUVWXYZ
abcdefghijklmnopqrstuvwxyz

Print script – British, 1920s to date

abcdefghijklmnopqrstuvwxyz
ABCDEFGHIJKLMNOPQR STUVWXYZ 1234567890

Italic, 1400s to date

From about 1880 there was strong German competition – a more theoretical and scientific approach from Dr Ludwig Klages, a philosopher, who co-founded the German Graphological Society in 1897, Dr William Preyer, a child psychiatrist, and Dr George Meyer, a psychiatrist. In 1904 the French and German schools of graphology split after arguments, and Klages went on to develop a deeper analysis, rather than just associating graphic signs with personality elements. He worked on the three aspects of each handwriting movement – speed, spacing and pressure.

A little later, between the two World Wars, Robert Saudek became a leading name in the field. He was a Czech who researched in Britain and the US, founded the first British journal of graphology (*Character and Personality*) and was particularly interested in the effects of speed on handwriting.

Another pioneer of this period was Max Pulver, a Swiss who worked with Dr Carl Jung; he wrote *Symbolism of Handwriting* (1931) and is particularly remembered for originating the three zones.

Hans Jacoby, from Germany, and Eric Singer, from Austria, escaped to Britain in 1936 and 1938 respectively to continue their researches. Jacoby's *Analysis of Handwriting* (1939) and Singer's *A Manual of Graphology* (1953) are both classics.

In the US, important early researchers included Louise Rice, who founded the American Graphological Society

Hans Jacoby (1906–45) escaped from Germany at the beginning of the First World War to continue his graphological researches. His *Analysis of Handwriting* (1939) is a classic.

in 1927, Jane Downey, Philip Vernon and Gordon Allport. They were followed in the 1940s by Thea Levinson and Joseph Zubin.

The acceptance of graphology as a science has meant that it is now studied at many universities as part of a degree in psychology.

The three zones

As your handwriting moves along, so it also moves up and down; this vertical movement is one of the important yardsticks of analysis. It was during the 1930s that the graphologist Max Pulver originated the idea of dividing handwriting into three vertical zones so that its relative size could be assessed.

The middle zone is defined as the area where the lower-case letters a, c, e, m, n, o, r, s, u, v, w and x are to be found. What we are interested in is how the height of these middle zone letters compares with the height of the upper and lower zone letters, in other words, their relative rather than their absolute size.

The upper zone will contain the upper parts of all capitals and of the following lower-case letters: b, d, h, k, l and t. The lower-case i is also included here because of its dot.

The lower zone will contain the lower parts of the lower-case letters g, j, p, q, y and (usually) z.

While every letter falls partly into the middle zone, the only letter to fall into all three zones, and the only one not so far listed, is the lower-case f.

The importance of the zones is that they stand for different aspects of the personality and that whichever zone is most prominent (largest) in handwriting will also tend to predominate in terms of personality.

upper zone
middle zone
lower zone

The zones

Upper zone. The spirit, the intellect, hopes, ideals, abstract things, speculations, ambitions.
Middle zone. The emotions, habits, social relationships, day-to-day behaviour, mundane things.
Lower zone. Sexual matters, instincts, urges, acquisition, possessiveness (material wealth), physical activities, the unconscious and drives in general.

Large upper zone: creative, imaginative,
enthusiastic.

*a small reading
breathing after en*

Small or absent lower zone: rather boring,
unimaginative, preoccupied by money
matters.

*and dolphins are nigl
rimals that live in us*

Large middle zone: egotistical, subjective,
lacking in self-criticism.

*have the anthology version that leaves out most
is cops down before the real report. I'll g*

Small middle zone: can imply obstinacy and
narrowness, but also drive, determination
and objectivity.

*Sorry I can't help
Frankly I had hardly heard o
so can only wish you both m*

Small lower zone: unpreoccupied by
matters sexual or financial.

*cleared annually in the early
made it was estimated that o*

Large lower zone: sensual, physically
active, tenacious; sometimes clumsy and
materialistic.

Upper zone analysis

Where the upper zone letters are relatively large and well developed this indicates great imagination, idealism, intelligence and enthusiasm. Full loops to the letters can suggest generosity. If the upper zone is exaggeratedly large at the expense of the other two zones one must beware of spiritual or intellectual ambitions taking over and the person mistaking fantasy for reality. This can also suggest extravagance, fanaticism and a general absence of objectivity. The self-confidence, drive and self-discipline necessary to carry plans through would probably be absent.

Middle zone analysis

A large middle zone indicates an excessive ego and some emotional instability. There may be a tendency towards subjectivity, exaggeration and excessive self-assertion; the person will be entirely lacking in self-criticism.

The ideal, a middle zone the same height as each of the other two zones, shows a well-balanced personality with self-confidence but also self-control.

If the middle zone is small it may indicate some pettiness or narrow-mindedness or even placid acceptance, but it is generally regarded as a good feature, suggesting objectivity, acute determination, attention to detail, modesty and ambition.

Lower zone analysis

A domination by the lower zone indicates practical concerns taking precedence. This will be a physically active person with a strong sex drive, a vigorous person who perseveres. The other side of the coin here may show a lack of imagination, some pedantry or clumsiness, perhaps an excessive sensuality and certainly excessive materialism.

Where this zone is small or absent there may well be a lack of materialism but also a lack of sexual drive, perhaps a lack of self-confidence and insufficient instinct for self-preservation.

Excessively long or ornate lower loops tend to suggest sexual fantasies or, at least, have some sexual significance that is capable of interpretation only in conjunction with other handwriting traits.

Slant

The slant is sometimes known as the letter slope or writing angle. At its most basic it indicates your personality type, with an extrovert having writing that slants to the right and an introvert having writing that slopes left.

There is a complicating factor at work here. The way in which you were taught to write at school is likely to have left its mark. For example, the Vere Foster method of writing was taught in Britain between about 1898 and the mid-1930s. Being a slight simplification of Copperplate, this involved a rightward slant of about 10° (that is, to 80°), which many children maintained into adult life and will practise today. This was succeeded by the Marion Richardson style, an upright form of writing with fuller, more rounded letters, which is in general still current (although some private schools teach a right-slanting Italic script).

In the US, different scripts are taught in different schools, but they all tend to have a right slant of 5° to 15°. The result is that most Americans write naturally with a right slant.

Upright

If your writing is upright or perpendicular, and regularly so, staying within about 93° to 87°, it indicates a controlled personality. (In fact, absolutely upright hand-

An upright style is often the product of an aloof, self-contained personality, who has an independence from the outside world.

15

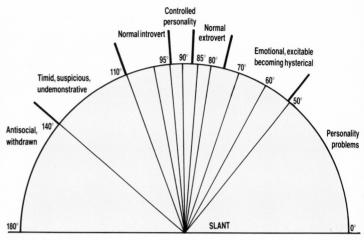

writing, or any perfectly consistent slope, is unusual.) You will tend to be a cool, restrained person who doesn't give in to emotions, who maintains an independence from the outside world. This may mean some degree of reserve or aloofness, a logical mind, impartiality and good judgement. It doesn't necessarily mean a lack of emotion or a standoffish attitude, though you are likely to be open with friends and acquaintances but politely formal towards strangers.

It seems that more men than women have upright handwriting.

Only if the writing is very upright and regular is there any cause for concern, as this may indicate an excess of egocentricity and strictness, and a lack of emotional response to others.

A normal right slant (top) suggests an active, broadminded, reasonably friendly and honest person. Where the slant is more pronounced (above), it implies someone who needs human contact more than most, and who is emotional and excitable.

Right slant

This is by far the most common slant amongst Americans, the British, other Europeans (not necessarily those writing in English) and even amongst people writing in different scripts, whether from left to right or right to left. If the slant is about 85° to 75° and is relatively consistent, not varying by more than about 5° from its average, it indicates a normal extrovert.

Most of us fall into this category. Symbolically this slant is a movement towards other people – an outgoing action. It suggests an active, demonstrative person who is willing to share thoughts and experiences, one who is naturally friendly, sympathetic, honest and broad-minded, all to a certain degree.

Where the right slant is excessive (even if it is regular), say in the range of 65° to 60°, the person is revealed as highly emotional, an excitable and enthusiastic extrovert who needs the company of others. As the slant increases more, say to 50°, so the personality is shown to be less restrained and more hysterical. Below 50° the person concerned may well have serious personality problems including total irresponsibility, aggressive tendencies and delusions of grandeur.

Left slant

Not only is this a relatively uncommon writing style, but it is one that owes nothing to any school teaching system and must be due solely to the individual's personality. Apart from anything else, it is difficult for right-handed writers to maintain a left slant since this is against the normal movement of the hand. The corollary of this is that it is slightly easier for left-handed writers to produce a left slant, though only by perhaps 5°, and few of them do so in practice.

Where a leftward slant is used it tends to be by introverts, who are inhibited, very cautious and modest, undemonstrative people. A large group with left-slant writing are teenagers, who try it out as a pose, and for whom it indicates a repressed or frustrated desire. Only a few post-teenagers persist with the style, and in older people it suggests disappointments, perhaps guilt feelings, a preference for the past rather than the future (of which there may be actual fear) and attitudes of defensiveness or suspicion. A man writing in this way may be fussy with a strongly developed feminine side to his character, while a woman may be thought cold and rather masculine in her approach.

Women are more likely than men to persist with a left slant throughout life.

An exaggerated left slant, more than 140°, suggests a withdrawal from normal society coupled with a general opposition to the ideas of others. This may lead to antisocial behaviour, a lack of friends and the writer becoming a social outcast.

Varying slant

Some natural variation of slant is only to be expected. Your mood or level of enthusiasm or the speed and degree of care with which you write will change from time to time. However, a regular fluctuation in slant suggests lack of control in the writer's personality.

This is not just a modern conclusion. Over 2,500 years ago Confucius the Chinese philosopher said that we should beware of people "whose writing is like a reed in the wind".

As with a leftward slant, significant variation is often met with in the writing of teenagers, who suffer from moodiness and insecurity as a by-product of growing up.

If the handwriting remains varying in slant into adulthood, it reveals an unpredictable personality, perhaps neurotic and unstable with basic conflicts unresolved. Look, in particular, for a leftward slant in just one of the writing zones. The degree of fluctuation will indicate the degree of unpredictability or instability.

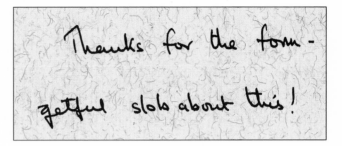

A leftward slant (above) is a sign of caution, modesty and an inhibited character. More pronounced (below), and the character traits are more markedly antisocial.

Slant variation (above) suggests a person at war with his or her own feelings, insecure and unstable. Such unresolved conflicts are often the result of an unhappy childhood. Sometimes (below), the variation is in one zone only.

General page layout

only recall a series of pictorial to achieve a good golfing star. holding my rod as though and I was about to charge.

Widely spaced writing: isolated, unhappy; shows one putting up barriers against human contact.

Always, even at school, had any trouble with it. Liked it. aged 11, the teacher was handu copying books to bad writers. them. Over a period of weeks deteriorated my writing. The gr

Normal line spacing: socially adept, well organized and balanced.

Line spacing

Most writers leave clear space between their lines. This "interlinear spacing" (to give it its proper name in graphology) will be influenced by several things, and a wide range of spacing may be regarded as acceptable.

A word of warning here if you are trying to analyse your own or anyone else's handwriting in this way: many people use lined paper as a matter of course, so they will be constrained by the existing lines. These may give spacing that is wide, narrow or just right depending upon their width and on the size of the person's writing. Where a person is asked to give a writing sample on an unlined sheet they may produce a variation of line spacing, however careful and methodical they are, simply through lack of practice – a reflection of the fact that people today are used to lined paper, typewriters or word processors.

The theory which governs the analysis of interlinear spacing is that it reflects the writer's ability to relate to his or her surroundings.

Very wide spacing is meant to show an isolated or unhappy individual who is using this space as a barrier. An emotional imbalance is indicated, giving rise to a lack of spontaneity or objectivity. Alternatively this may just be the result of a lack of concentration, so that the writer progresses extremely slowly. Wide spacing also suggests a childlike personality.

Where the lines are evenly spaced the writer is generally regarded as well-balanced, socially adept, and an excellent organizer with a good sense of direction.

Overlapping lines, with almost no space between them so that the upper zone of one line interferes with the lower zone of another, suggests a muddled thinker. Apart from the added difficulty of reading such writing, it may indicate a very impulsive writer, perhaps even somebody with mental problems.

Where the line spacing varies, there may be a number of causes. Unfamiliarity with writing on unlined paper and a desire for thrift (narrower lines towards the bottom of a page to avoid beginning another sheet are common) are possibilities. It may suggest a writer with poor judgement, a careless attitude to life, and problems with conversation and self-expression. Such a person is likely to be erratic in social situations, too.

Word spacing

The spaces you leave between the words you write are generally indicative of your organizational abilities. Normal spacing between words depends upon the size of your writing, so cannot easily be expressed in absolute terms, such as millimetres. It may, however, be defined as the width of 1½ to 2 of your more rounded letters (a, e, o). This is regarded as ideal because it is enough to separate the words so that they can easily be distinguished, but not so much as to slow down the reader.

Most people, who have balanced judgement, relatively clear thinking, warmth, self-assurance and good social skills, write with normal spacing most of the time (though extreme haste may cause words to run into each other).

Where the spacing is narrow, the writer is displaying a need for social contact, impatience, impulsiveness, a lack of inhibitions and is somewhat lacking in tact, critical skills or normal social abilities. There may also be some lack of organizational skills.

If the words actually run into each other, so that deciphering them is a great trial, then the conditions or traits listed in the last paragraph are present in the extreme. For example, there may be a desperate drive for social

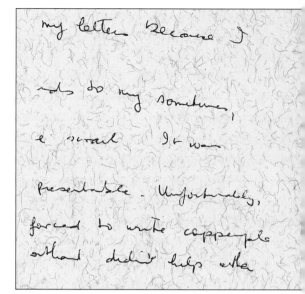

Varying line spacing: irresponsible, devil-may-care.

Overlapping lines: tends to denote muddled thinking.

Normal word spacing: warm, self-assured, clear-thinking.

Narrow word spacing: a tendency to be lonely, impatient, tactless and impulsive.

Margins

The most noticeable feature of a page of writing is the white space – or lack of white space – around it. While certain personality traits may be assumed from these margins, it is important not to read too much into them, since there are numerous reasons why a person will choose particular widths of margin.

One factor is nationality (or, rather, the country of your schooling). In North and South America, children are normally taught not to use margins at all. In Britain, children are taught to write using a left-hand margin of about two-fingers' width. Many children try to maintain this in adulthood because it looks natural to them. And in continental Europe, though teaching varies, school-book margins that are wider than British ones are often insisted on.

Another factor is economy, or thrift. The Protestant ethic of "waste not, want not" is often applied to paper use, with the thrifty writer leaving narrow margins, if any, and then perhaps adding a line or two in the margins rather than beginning a fresh sheet.

Paper size is a third factor. The person who normally leaves wide margins all round their writing when using A4 may well do without margins entirely if writing in a small notebook or on a postcard. Or a person who normally fills a sheet of writing-paper (A5 or smaller) without margins may feel intimidated by the extra space when asked to write on A4, and will therefore leave wide margins in an attempt to cover the same number of pages as usual.

A final factor is the reason why one is writing. A casual letter to a friend will be written with less care as to margins than will a letter of application for a job. It is important to know the writer's profession and reason for writing, as well as his or her country of schooling.

Despite all these warnings, there are character conclusions that may be drawn from a person's use of margins.

The theory is that the left-hand side of the page symbolizes the past and the right-hand side the future. Narrow left-hand margins are meant to reflect insecurity, stand-offishness and a lack of organizational ability (especially if the lines or letters are crammed together), together with a need for popularity and acceptance, while a wide left-hand margin indicates a friendly, generous person who may well be reserved and uncaring of the past.

More useful for analysis purposes is the left-hand margin that widens, narrows or varies from line to line. Any deviation from the original chosen margin indicates a lack of control – either through thinking faster than your writing speed or through changes of mood. A widening left-hand margin is most indicative of impatience to get the piece of writing finished. A narrowing left-hand margin (somewhat rare) can suggest secret fears, shyness and guilt. Where the left-hand margin is haphazard, so is the person's mind likely to be, either through a lack of care, a lack of education or perhaps a lack of artistic awareness.

Right-hand margins are more difficult still to analyse because variations in word length will make even the most orderly writer produce a slight unevenness. It is claimed that, all other things being equal, a wide right-hand margin indicates shyness or fear or suspicion, while a narrow one indicates good powers of communication and co-operation.

The upper margin is important. The writer's first mark on the page (known as the "entrance") is often a good indicator of personality. The friendly communicator (extrovert) will most often begin closer to the top of the page and to the left-hand side, while the shy outsider (introvert) will begin further down and in. A very wide or very narrow upper margin (and certainly a cramped lower margin) will indicate poor planning ability in the writer. Obviously, the confident and well-organized writer is more likely to achieve an attractive final result with equal and even margins all round the page. If this is done with very wide margins all round it may mean that the writer is vain or a poseur, trying to suggest an impression of importance and artistic appreciation.

Once again it is necessary to stress that no one particular factor should be examined in isolation. The overall look and balance of the page (including letter, word and line spacing, paragraphing and general consistency) is a much more important indicator than any single width of margin. And the external factors must always be considered, too.

---

1 Lack of top margin: reflects direct, informal, perhaps disrespectful person; lack of bottom margin: dreamy and sentimental. 2 Large top margin: signifies reserved and formal writer; a large bottom margin indicates one with a superficial manner. 3 No margins: obsessional about money and financial security.

4 Wide margins: isolated, private, possibly prone to morbid anxiety. 5 Wide left margin: shy, but generous towards others. 6 Small right margin: gregarious, full of vitality and courage, but inclined to act hastily; 7 Irregular left margin: moody, indecisive, inconsistent and often fearful.

contact – the writer wants to be identified with a group but cannot. The personality is unstable.

If the opposite is the case, with words sitting isolated, separated by word-sized gaps, then the writer is displaying an excessive reserve. He or she will tend to be a shy and lonely introvert, perhaps conceited, perhaps very critical of others, and either unable or unwilling to interact with others. Thinking will be undisciplined, though such a person may possess good artistic abilities. Wide word spacing often begins in adolescence, where some sense of shyness and aloofness is a common stage. Usually this is a passing phase. Occasionally, widely spaced writing is adopted as an artistic-seeming pose.

Again, really excessively wide spacing can denote an unstable personality.

Even more instability is shown by irregular word spacing. This may be caused by mood fluctuations, from introversion to extroversion, as in manic depression.

Letter spacing

This can be analysed in a similar way to word spacing. Average or normal letter spacing has a gap (not a clear gap, usually, but one containing a connecting stroke) of about half the width of a round letter.

Narrower letter spacing can indicate deficiencies in adaptability, concentration and discipline. Where this is excessive, with the letters overlapping, you can suspect a disturbed personality with symptoms of anxiety, impulsiveness, egocentricity and great selfishness.

Wider than normal letter spacing is not necessarily indicative of any personality defects. Certainly the writing will be easily read. It suggests an open, alert and frank person with good imagination and creativity. Only when taken to extremes (or found in conjunction with other symptoms) is it possible to diagnose a lack of adaptability, weakness of concentration, an easily provoked irritation and hysteria.

The irregular, looping strokes between letters here suggest great energy and enthusiasm, and perhaps showmanship. Their unusual and self-conscious appearance implies someone who is rebellious. In a slower, less fluent and rhythmic style, they might well be considered to be pauses for thought.

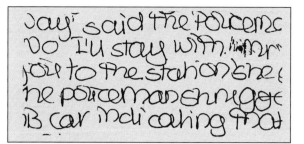

Very narrow word spacing: possibly unstable, implying desperate need for human contact.

Wide word spacing: hypercritical, introverted and arrogant.

Irregular word spacing: indicative of mood swings.

Narrow letter spacing: rigid, undisciplined, unable to concentrate.

Very narrow letter spacing: indicates desire to conceal one's true feelings.

Wide letter spacing: open, alert and candid.

Very wide letter spacing: undisciplined, over-emotional, liable to flare up.

Irregular letter spacing: rebellious, energetic and flamboyant.

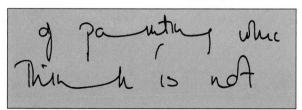

Size and alignment

> *Ike ground involve*
> *1, recognisable object*
> *valve à liberal am*

A normal size implies someone who is fair-minded and who can see an argument from all sides.

> *Enclosed is my offer*
> *Anniversary Book*
> *of few of my Mon*

Larger than average writing has good and bad sides: imagination and enthusiasm, but also pomposity and a sense of self-importance.

Very large writing often means a total self-absorption on the writer's part.

> *ik you for asking r*
> *sample, I don't t*

Size

The overall size of handwriting varies enormously, and the most important conclusion to be drawn from this is the subjectivity or objectivity of the writer.

Normal-sized writing is about 3 mm high in each of the three zones. In other words, an "a" will be 3 mm high, a "t" 6 mm high and an "f" 9 mm high.

Large writing (over 3 mm in each zone) indicates a subjective personality. This is a person believing in their own self-importance, probably proud, enthusiastic, outgoing, active and imaginative. It may perhaps be a person who is an exhibitionist, one who always exaggerates, who lacks caution or control, who is jealous and impulsive. Such professionals as film stars and pop musicians, whose egocentricity is often a necessary and sufficient cause of their success, tend to have large handwriting. So, also, do children – which just goes to show the childish nature of egocentric people.

In extreme cases, the writer will be totally self-centred and self-absorbed with a leaning towards megalomania.

Small handwriting (under 3 mm in each zone) denotes an objective personality. There is modesty, shrewdness, good concentration, good self-control, attention to detail and a sense of realism. Such people tend to include scientists, philosophers and any type of theoretician (as opposed to people of action) amongst their numbers. There may be some negative traits including pedantry, pettiness, miserliness, a lack of emotion and no zest for life.

Very small handwriting suggests an inferiority complex – a poor self-image. It may also accompany hypochondria.

The size of handwriting is often uneven; it varies regularly within words. In particular, the beginnings or endings of words are written larger or smaller than the rest. This is a reflection of the writer's self-image.

Larger initial letters (especially capitals) denote arrogance, conceit, great self-awareness and ambition, which are often accompanied by talkativeness and a need to be seen by others.

On the other hand, relatively small initial letters are indicative of modesty, humility, genuine regard for others, and perhaps a low self-esteem or feelings of insecurity.

Where it is the word endings which are particularly enlarged or fancy, the person will be open and generous but also ambitious, persuasive and egocentric.

Smaller than normal endings suggest a tactful and courteous person, perhaps shy and self-effacing, certainly cautious and adaptable. This may also be a person unwilling to be committed to anything and unnecessarily suspicious.

Small writing (left) tends to suggest a modest, shrewd person with good self-control; very small writing (below) is often the result of a poor self-image.

An enlarged word ending (above) is the product of a showy, rather self-centred, but often generous writer; by contrast, a small word ending (left) implies a cautious, self-effacing person.

★ STAR SIGNS ★ STAR SIGNS ★ S

Neil Armstrong

The first man on the Moon has a showy signature, intended to grab the attention. The large, fairly ornate capitals and the double flourish beneath are the marks of a show-off who may be self-centred and even vain, but who also certainly possesses a sense of the dramatic.

All the qualities one would expect to find in an astronaut are suggested by the precise, upright writing style with careful dot-placing and a long t-bar. These are: precision, a good memory, a great capacity for hard work, the ability to plan ahead and to proceed in a slow and methodical manner. There is a touch of the perfectionist and the suggestion of great ambition, too.

The very narrow letter spacing is a negative aspect, suggesting a lack of adaptability, while the very tall upper zone could indicate strong intellectual and spiritual concerns that might interfere with the job in hand.

Richard Nixon (signature)

Richard Nixon

The most surprising aspects of this signature are those we don't see: no signs of either great leadership potential or deceit.

Here is an outgoing person with the right-slanting style that virtually all US presidents have had. There is openness in his wide letter spacing, consideration for others in his simple, easily read signature and a friendly informality in the way he omits his middle name entirely. Clearly he is a fast thinker, and if there is ambition to be seen in the width of the letters and some degree of showing off in the large, broad capitals, this is to be expected. The largish writing does not necessarily indicate vanity.

Alignment

Also known as direction or slope (not to be confused with slant), this refers to whether your written lines are horizontal or not. The most normal cause of any deviation from the horizontal is the writer's mood, which may vary almost minute by minute, having an immediate and visible effect. If you check samples of your handwriting from different times you will probably find quite a variation in alignment. Obviously this is more noticeable when a person is writing on unlined paper, but there are tendencies to look for and conclusions to be drawn even from writing done on lined paper.

Keeping your writing absolutely horizontal on unlined paper is difficult, requiring tremendous amounts of unvarying concentration. If you see an example of this you must suspect that the writer has used a guide – a lined sheet placed underneath the page he or she was writing on so that the lines showed through.

Horizontal writing (even with small variations in alignment) signifies a reliable, stable person with a methodical approach to life and plenty of self-control. The negative side of such qualities is that the person may be entirely unemotional to the point of unapproachability, also dull and inflexible and so over-controlled that this may be a defensive posture.

It is quite common for a line of writing to ascend slightly from left to right. This is generally expressive of

Suffolk is well endowed musically so I imbi Remit. Snape is gloriously just up the road, many churches where music sacred and profan oral concert facilities. Local Wolsey Theatre

Horizontal/no slant: methodical, reliable, stable.

there's no doubt about it if you want to influence people when

Rising line: energetic, creative, optimistic.

ould think of, nd the right ideas itable for the book. d a use for them, keep it in the smalles

Falling line: indicative of tiredness, depression, pessimism and, possibly, ill-health.

a buoyant, enthusiastic mood. It tends to suggest a happy, optimistic individual with plenty of creativity and drive. Also, a rising line is unlikely to be repeated exactly in lines above and below. Sometimes the level of enthusiasm varies according to the particular words being written (a professional writer is elated by the phrase he or she has just thought of, or a letter-writer is describing an especially happy memory). Occasionally the enthusiasm becomes excessive and the line of writing rises at a steeper angle, suggesting an impulsive nature, a frivolous mood, or even the presence of hysteria.

A gradually descending line may denote the opposite – some pessimism or depression. Or it may be an indicator of tiredness (the enthusiastic optimist at the end of a hard day), or illness (even a slight debilitation that has not yet produced symptoms of physical pain may affect the alignment of your handwriting), or of old age. In extreme cases of physical or mental illness (or severe but temporary fatigue) the downward slope may be exaggerated.

Sometimes it is only the last word or two on the line that descend. Various explanations may account for this, including feelings of tiredness or aggression, or a disorganized and time-wasting character.

Another variation is where the words on the line ascend or descend in a step-like or tile-like fashion (each word level but higher or lower than the previous word). Rising steps suggest curbed enthusiasm, something held back and a need for release. Descending steps are indicative of a struggle against tiredness or depression or a lack of self-confidence; there may be a fear of failure inherent in this.

Most of us write in rather wavy lines from time to time, but if this trait is frequent or pronounced, it is an indicator of indecision, moodiness and instability, or possibly of sensitivity and imagination.

If a line both rises and falls, it may still tell the graphologist something useful about the writer. A convex line may simply reflect fatigue, or it may mean a lack of enthusiasm or a lack of persistence. A concave line can show weariness, self-doubt or depression, but it may equally well denote an increase in effort or enthusiasm by a person reaching for a goal.

Upward steps: a need to relieve pent-up tension.

Downward steps: a battle against shyness and depression.

Convex line: reflects a lack of enthusiasm or sticking power.

Concave line: suggests someone with self-doubt, depression, or one straining after a goal.

When writing on lined paper, the person who persistently writes exactly on the line may be seen as highly disciplined but perhaps lacking in independence and unable to make decisions. Writing above the line shows independence and enthusiasm, though perhaps also an innate stubbornness and the lack of a sense of reality. A person who writes consistently below the printed line (so that letters repeatedly cross the line) has a strongly developed sense of reality and a concern for material possessions, yet may lack enthusiasm and concentration.

In view of the frequency with which our writing changes alignment and the large number of relevant factors at work here, it would be unwise to analyse any handwriting sample on this basis alone.

25

Pressure

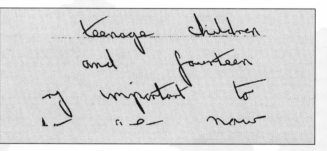

Writers tend to reflect their energy level and perhaps their degree of concentration in the pressure they exert in pushing the pen into the paper. This is most evident on the reverse side of the sheet of paper.

Normally you will find yourself using more pressure in downstrokes than in upstrokes or horizontals. This, again, can be best seen on the reverse of the sheet.

A factor to beware of (when trying to analyse pressure) is the writing implement used. Fountain-pens, ball-points and pencils allow an analysis of pressure; felt-tips and roller-balls usually do not. Note that some broad-nibbed pens may give a false impression of pressure because of the amount of ink on the page.

Heavy pressure (below) can imply stubbornness or aggression. Where the downstrokes alone are heavy (above), this is a sign of egotism.

Heavy pressure

This normally reveals an energetic, positive nature. However, it may just be that the writer is concentrating greatly (unused to writing, perhaps) or is under stress, and here the style will appear slow and deliberate. Where heavy pressure is combined with regular flow it suggests energy and self-confidence – a person who approaches all aspects of life with lots of vitality.

On the other hand, if only the downstrokes are heavy, the writer may be egotistical. Heavy pressure can indicate aggression, obstinacy or the presence of inhibitions.

Medium pressure

This reveals less about the personality than either heavy or light pressure, especially if the medium pressure is regular. It shows reasonable control, a constructive use of energy and moderate determination.

Light pressure

This may indicate a delicate, sensitive person, possibly introverted. If the writing is small and light it suggests a scientific bent; when the writing is large it suggests that the person is relatively undisciplined.

Very light pressure

Extreme sensitivity is suggested here. Perhaps the person is timid or lacking in energy, though tact, modesty and tolerance are also indicated. In particularly extreme cases there may be a lack of enthusiasm, of initiative and of sexual energy.

Pastose writing

Literally, the word means "full of paint" and indicates a thick line of writing softly applied as if by a brush. It refers to simulated heavy pressure through the use of a broad nib lightly used. The individual is likely to be of an artistic type, warm and emotional, full of ideas.

Varying pressure

This means an almost random fluctuation in pressure, not a regular variation (or "shading") between downstrokes and upstrokes. It may manifest itself as occasional heavy strokes in light script or as occasional light strokes in heavy script. Either way, it indicates instability – the writer may have a violent nature and little control, or may be insecure. Watch for variation in only one of the zones.

Very light writing: extremely sensitive, tolerant, perhaps timid.

Pastose writing: warm, emotional, imaginative.

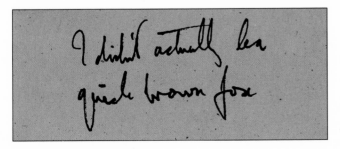

Varying pressure: insecure, hot-tempered.

Shading

This terms refers to the relative heaviness of upstrokes and downstrokes. Although it is connected with pressure it should be regarded as a separate point of analysis. It may be thought of as an indicator of sensuality. Fountain-pens, felt-tips, roller-balls, and pencils can be used to show shading, while ball-points usually cannot.

Shading is normally considered according to the thickness of the stroke. Strokes are either sharp or pastose.

Sharp strokes

The sharp stroke is a thin one. There is no width difference between upstrokes and downstrokes, and the actual pressure used tends to be on the weak side of medium. All beginning and ending strokes, whichever zone they are in, have a sharp look to them. The people who write like this are non-sensual. They are often determined, idealistic, self-disciplined and purposeful individuals with good thought-processes. They can also be quick to criticize and cold, narrow-minded and acerbic, even quarrelsome.

Pastose strokes

The pastose stroke, as mentioned above, is thick, resembling a brush stroke, yet it is normally achieved without much pressure. The secret here is free-flowing ink. Again, stroke width does not vary much between upstrokes and downstrokes. Pastose writers are very sensual people. Indeed, they may be too much dominated by their senses. They are warm, pleasure-loving people, who appreciate beauty, possess great imagination and are both willing and able to enjoy intense experiences. At the same time they can lack spirituality, can be lazy or self-indulgent, and can lack moral self-control.

If you want to produce thinner upstrokes and wider downstrokes you will need to employ a broader nib and write more slowly and carefully. This is half-way to being a form of calligraphy, and its lack of spontaneity shows in the writer's character, too. This sort of writer will tend to be artistic and moral, with a well-developed sense of duty.

Connecting strokes

Most handwriting is connected up. Indeed, it is worth remembering that printed script (writing that is not joined up) cannot be analysed at all. There are just four basic types of connecting stroke: angular, arcade, garland and thread, though each of these contains a wide range of variation. While any handwriting style will mostly reflect one of the four, it is common for elements of another to be present as well.

The significance of these connecting strokes is that they tend to reflect the writer's social attitudes.

Angular connections: stable, reliable, well-motivated; too rigid at times.

Arcade connections: secretive, critical, traditional, solitary.

Garland connections: tolerant, extrovert, lacking in will-power.

Angular

In its purest form this reveals a highly disciplined and purposeful individual – stable, reliable and well motivated. Going hand in hand with this is a tendency to be too rigid and stubborn, caring more about getting the job done than about relationships or teamwork.

Arcade

The arch shape symbolizes the way in which this type of writer is secretive, trying to cover his or her own writing to prevent it from being seen by others. Here is a person who is reserved and cautious, rather formal and sensitive, who tends to be traditional and to prefer being alone. Negative traits include suspicion of others, a lack of sincerity, a rigid mind closed to new ideas and a critical, anti-social outlook on the world.

Garland

The smooth flow of motion in this writing symbolizes adaptability and openness – the opposite of arcade. These people are tolerant, sympathetic and socially outgoing. On the other hand, they may be too easily influenced by others, their weaker will-power means that they are subject to distractions, are often changeable and may become dependent upon others.

Thread

The rather straggling connections here conceal an agile and instinctive mind. This is the person who avoids authority and dislikes rulebooks, but is clever enough to succeed in his or her own fashion. There is a tendency towards instability or insecurity, and some of the person's original ideas will be too high-flown or impractical to be worth considering. In an extreme case a hysterical personality is denoted.

Thread connections: rebellious, independent, instinctive.

Four connection types

ANGULAR	/\/\/\/\/
ARCADE	⌒⌒⌒⌒
GARLAND	\/\/\/\/
THREAD	⌒∿∿∿.

Unconnected writing

The relatively small number of people who write in an unlinked script are supposed to possess a sense of artistic appreciation or awareness that makes them see letters as parts of a drawing. This does not necessarily mean that they have a talent for drawing or painting. Such people tend to concentrate on small details rather than on the whole. They can be fussy and good at finding fault, but they can also be creatively original.

who is coming

No connections: fussy about details, but also artistic.

Initial strokes

This refers to the lead-in stroke at the beginning of each word. It is a useful indicator of the writer's preparation for writing. Generally speaking, a long lead-in stroke indicates a slower thinker, though the shape and position of the stroke are also important.

It must be noted that there are wide national differences here, due to different styles of lead-in stroke being taught in schools in the US and continental Europe.

Some slow and deliberate thinkers may use not only a long initial stroke but also one or more "feeling strokes", which involve touching the paper with the pen without actually writing a letter or word. This is a sort of trial run, usually very faint, and it is the mark of an unsure writer, often lacking in determination, self-confidence and perhaps the ability to order his or her thoughts.

Long initial strokes denote the preparation time needed by the writer, but the speed of writing must be taken into account. In slow writing it does suggest a slow and deliberate thinker, a time-waster, a person who looks to others for reassurance, a follower of rules.

Alternatively, in fast writing the lead-in may just be the writer getting up speed, even if the stroke is very long and starts in the lower zone.

A lower zone beginning in slow writing indicates a fixation on the past (the past is always to the left of your writing and the future to the right).

Long lead-in stroke

Ornate lead-in stroke

Lead-in stroke from beneath the base line

Ornate terminal stroke

Where the lead-in strokes are always hooked it suggests a persistent individual who may be irascible.

If the lead-in is ornate, particularly where it originates in the upper zone, it indicates a poseur, a show-off, perhaps a person trying to appear artistic or sensitive. On the other hand, the Palmer script, taught in the US, features some fairly ornate lead-in strokes, so the graphologist must be careful here.

Where the initial stroke always begins on the base line (the bottom of the middle zone, often the line printed on the paper) it suggests a person who is happy to obey authority and always be a follower, someone who will conform and be methodical without making decisions or deviating. This is something that frequently accompanies a copybook writing style.

An absence of lead-in strokes indicates a person who gets on with things at once, a quick thinker, one who is mature, decisive, intelligent, perhaps with originality and flair.

But even without a lead-in stroke, there may be visible hesitancy on the initial stroke – a wiggle, or something similar, suggesting a degree of indecision.

Terminal strokes

The final or end movement, concluding a word, is very revealing. It suggests how the writer relates to the future and how he or she gets on with other people. There is a mood element here too, so some frequent variation may be expected. Speed is another relevant factor, since it is almost impossible for a fast writer to stop dead at the end of a word.

If forgery or fraud is suspected, the terminal stroke is one of the most telling clues. It is very difficult for a forger (who usually writes relatively slowly) to make his or her hand do the same when coming to rest as the original writer (who probably wrote more quickly) did automatically.

Where there is an absence of a terminal stroke, it may suggest a careful, self-controlled person, perhaps direct and mistrustful of others, perhaps one who doesn't bother too much with politeness. If the last letter is incomplete it suggests these things more strongly – selfishness, rudeness, perhaps even loneliness.

Hooked lead-in stroke

Lead-in from the base line

Incomplete last letter

Different terminal strokes

Liberal attitudes, spontaneity, unafraid of a challenge.

would

Great enthusiasm for the subject being written about; haste.

of mine

Suspicious, determined, even curious.

have

Brutal or possessive.

are

Weak or timid.

come

Defensive or self-protective.

the

Mystical.

ask

Literary, poetic, imaginative, or just a poseur.

your

Terminal stroke: down and to the right

Any hooks on terminal strokes indicate an irritable, contentious type of person.

If the stroke goes on down and to the right it suggests selfishness and reticence. If it continues below the base line it is a sign of unfriendliness or intolerance.

Where the stroke returns to the left, running through the last letter of the word, it suggests that the writer is untrusting and introverted.

If the ending is a point, then the writer is said to have a strong sense of purpose.

An ending in an extreme curve means someone who pays great attention to detail.

A slight upward curve suggests generosity, while a bigger upward curve denotes a person who is shy and self-conscious.

Terminal stroke with hook

Terminal/below the base line

Speed, regularity and rhythm

Fast writing, not surprisingly, suggests an agile, spontaneous mind.

A slow writer is generally more methodical and thorough, but may be more passive.

Speed

Most people have an optimum or favourite speed at which they normally write. This tends to reflect the speed at which they think and the speed at which they live their life. In other words, a quick writer will probably possess mental agility, spontaneity, adaptability, vitality, enthusiasm and a tendency towards extroversion. On the other hand, he or she could be excitable, shallow, rash, easily influenced, lacking in concentration and lacking in the ability to analyse and plan.

A slow writer is likely to be methodical, steady and thoughtful, thorough and precise, but may be over-cautious, passive, lazy and lacking in intelligence.

But how can you tell (without watching them) how fast a person writes? The answer is that there are many features to look out for.

(a) *i-dots and t-strokes*. In slow writing these are precisely placed or even, occasionally, shifted to the left; also, a break is often visible where the writer stopped, directly after writing the i or t, to form the dot or bar. In fast writing they will most often be placed to the right, will sometimes be connected to following letters, and may occasionally be omitted. There will be no break after the letter because the dot or bar will almost always be added at the end of the word.

(b) *Left margin.* If this is maintained accurately or if it narrows going down the page, slow writing is indicated. If it widens or varies, the writing has been fast.

(c) *Slant.* This is almost always rightward and consistent in fast writing; it may be leftward and inconsistent in slow writing.

(d) *Pressure.* This is consistent in fast writing and tends to be average or light; in slow writing there is more variation and more pressure.

(e) *Connection.* Where letters are unconnected or the form of connection is angular or arcade, slow writing is indicated; in fast writing the letters are fully connected, most often by garlands or threads. Some words may be linked, too.

(f) *End strokes.* In slow writing these may be blunt and will often be produced by leftward movements. In fast writing the endings will be to the right.

(g) *Simplicity.* The simplest styles of letter formation may not necessarily indicate fast writing, but any complicated or ornamented styles will point to slow writing.

(h) *Firmness.* In general, a firm stroke suggests fast writing and a broken or shaky line suggests slow speed.

(i) *Width.* Narrow letters and narrow spacing are indicative of slow speed; broader letters and spacing suggest fast writing.

(j) *Word endings.* If these are exaggerated, suspect slow writing; if they get smaller, this suggests fast writing.

(k) *Rhythm.* There is a rhythmic flow to fast writing which cannot be achieved at a slower pace – even though slow writing tends to be more precise and regular.

As the pace of writing can be deceptive, it is wise to study all these factors and never to come to a conclusion on the basis of just one or two.

Legibility

If handwriting is to be useful it must be legible; legibility is most often linked to speed. Whenever writers try to increase their speed, legibility will suffer. Certainly, slow handwriting is almost always easily read, while some fast writing is illegible. There is no real connection between legibility and intelligence. Nor is there a clear connection between legibility and personality type,

Freddie Mercury

The lead singer of the rock group, Queen, he died in late 1991 of AIDS. This signature is a combination of haste, sensitivity and sensuality, which seem to sum up his public persona exactly. The haste is in the missing letters, the sensitivity is in the stunted d-loops and the sensuality is in that enormous y-loop.

The large capital letters are what one would expect from such a showman; the F being larger than the M merely indicates a wish for informality. The very long lead-in stroke to the M just signifies a fast writer getting up speed.

Writing that has very poor form, and is difficult to read, can be a subconscious attempt at concealment.

Retouched letters can be the action of one who is eager to please, nervous and unselfconfident.

though it has been suggested that an illegible style is an attempt by the writer (perhaps even unconsciously) to deceive or to hide something.

A slow, clear style of writing, especially if very close to that learnt in school, suggests a plodder, possibly lacking in education and/or self-confidence. Such a person may be unhappy writing anything down, yet is likely to be a good, methodical worker in routine jobs.

A shaky style of writing may indicate that a person is elderly, physically weak or ill, perhaps a sufferer from Parkinson's disease or some other ataxic disorder, a mentally unstable person, or somebody attempting fraud or deceit by adopting an unfamiliar style.

Where the writer has obviously retouched a lot of letters or strokes, it suggests that he or she is trying to be too hasty in his or her writing and yet is anxious that the words should be legible. This may be due to nervousness, an attempt to make a good impression, or to an attempt to make reality match his or her hopes. In any case, there will probably be a lack of self-confidence.

Regularity

The regularity of a writing sample can be checked by examining:

(a)   The heights of the middle zone letters.
(b)   The positioning of downstrokes (as compared with the letters of which they are part).
(c)   The consistency of the slant.
(d)   The line spacing.

Very regular writing is generally easy to spot due to its pattern. Regular writing is a mark of a stable person who doesn't object to mundane activities and is calm, methodical and reliable. The person may also be boring and unemotional.

If it is very regular, the writer will be conscientious, predictable and inflexible, unimaginative, perhaps slow, perhaps lacking in vitality, perhaps compulsive in habits.

Most handwriting is slightly irregular, with one or two of these four factors showing variation. Such writers are flexible and balanced people. They don't lack emotional response but are in control of it.

A very regular hand shows the writer is rather inflexible and slow, whilst being dependable and predictable.

Irregular writers (with three or four factors showing) have little emotional control, are excitable, easily confused by awkward or novel situations, moody and restless, and are not contented people. But they may also be lively and creative, very flexible, passionate and open-minded in outlook.

Very irregular writers (with all four factors showing) may be imaginative, inventive and artistic, but also intolerant of routine or stress. If writing pressure is inconsistent it suggests that they are easily distracted, wasteful of time, easily dominated, seldom satisfied, inconsistent and irrational in their behaviour and confused in their thinking.

Rhythm

The experienced graphologist can tell a great deal about a person from the rhythm of his or her writing. This is not an easy skill; it must be learnt and comes only with long practice.

Put simply, a good rhythm in handwriting is where the style is regular without being forced, where the script is simple and legible, and where the writer is obviously relaxed (the pressure is neither heavy nor light) and has good pen control. It is possible to hold a sample of rhythmic handwriting upside-down or sideways or look at its reflection in a mirror and still see the regularity. But you must beware of excessive regularity, indicating a forced rhythm, which will probably be accompanied by heavy pressure.

A regular rhythm shows the writer to be of good physical and mental health, possessing self-control, self-discipline and will-power, reliable, tolerant of pressure, with good concentration and a sense of purpose, and possessing an inner tranquillity. There may perhaps be a lack of spontaneity and of emotional warmth.

If the writing is excessively regular this means that the writer is putting too much effort into it. This pressure and rigidity suggests a degree of self-control and self-discipline that interferes with the personality, sapping vitality and suppressing emotional response, creativity and the capacity to change. Such a person will be very reserved and restrained in behaviour patterns and may be afflicted by compulsive behaviour.

Very irregular writers tend to be artistic and passionate, but intolerant of rules and easily distracted.

A regular, flowing style is redolent of spiritual and bodily health.

There are different ways in which writing may be lacking in rhythm. Sometimes there is inconsistency due to over-fast writing (the result of impatience, usually) and sometimes there is hesitancy due to a lack of practice at writing or to some problem of poor health or disability. Some writing that lacks rhythm may still possess an inner harmony, suggesting an individual who prefers not to conform yet possesses creativity and vitality.

Poor rhythm means an irregular style – ugly-looking writing. This can signify emotional sensitivity, great powers of imagination, adaptability and impulsiveness. It can also indicate insecurity, moodiness, a nervous temperament and a lack of reliability.

There is also the case of a disturbed rhythm, where the person has emotional problems, is subject to swift mood changes, is unable to cope with internal conflicts and will probably be full of complaints about life. Here the writing has no pattern to it at all, but varies all the time in size, layout, slant and spacing. It will probably include crossings out and retouched letters.

Tension and release

It is inevitable that we will be affected by feelings of tension from time to time, and equally inevitable that these will show themselves in our handwriting. Quite possibly the subject of the writing will be to blame – a letter of resignation or a lie being told.

The degree of tension and of release are both mentally controlled. They are achieved via the extensor muscles, which extend the fingers, and the flexor muscles, which draw in the fingers. This drawing in causes tension, while an extension relaxes. If the writer feels tense, the writing will tend to be more regular, smaller and slower than normal, with heavy pressure and disconnected and narrow letters. Any connections will probably be angular or arcade, with a reduced middle zone, narrow spacing, a downward slope to lines and a more leftward slant than normal.

The first sample (A) shows a relaxed and upright style, which gradually becomes smaller, more leftward slanting and a little less connected further down the sheet (B). The writer's tension is only released in the last line (C) because he knows he has almost finished the letter.

Poor rhythm: haste

Poor rhythm: irregular style

Poor rhythm: disturbed personality

Normal... A

Tension... B

Release C

Individual letters

Width of letters

The width of letters reflects the writer's social attitudes – narrow letters mean a reserved person, wide letters an outgoing one – and is closely connected with the degree of slant. (See pages 13 to 15.)

The normal or ideal is for the middle zone letters to be as wide as they are tall, so that a narrow letter is noticeably narrower than this and a wide letter noticeably wider.

Narrow writing tends to obstruct the normal left to right movement of the act of writing. It is obvious that the narrower the writing the less easy it will be to read; downstrokes will become covering strokes. Also, the narrower the writing the greater the degree of introversion on the part of the writer. Narrow writers are, on the whole, reserved people, perhaps shy and unemotional. They may be very practical, tactful and dependable, with good powers of concentration and a useful sense of economy. They will be realists, modest with a good sense of control and balanced judgement. On the other hand, they tend to be narrow-minded, perhaps distrustful, selfish and intolerant. In extreme cases, the narrow writer will have a hefty inferiority complex, will avoid all social contact, and will be argumentative and spiteful. These tendencies are more pronounced where there is also a leftward slant.

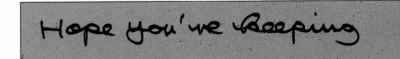

Narrow writing (above) often signifies a reserved, upright but trustworthy peson, while the widely spaced letters (below) belong to a generous, frank, but possibly arrogant person.

Wide writing is characteristic of the expansive, outgoing personality. This is a spontaneous, emotional person who is social, frank and generous. Wide writing shows ambition, good organizing ability, sincerity and a consistency of purpose. But he or she may also be tactless and reckless, lacking in self-control, reserve and discipline. This may be a very demanding person, impatient, superficial and arrogant. One thing about wide writing is that it is almost always easy to read, because the letters are not only broad but spaced out.

Punctuation

Several important traits show themselves in the use of punctuation marks, though the subject itself is not important enough for conclusions to be drawn unless they are backed up by other evidence.

Where punctuation is lacking, the writer is (unless he or she is simply ignorant of the rules of grammar) lacking in attention to detail. We use commas and full stops to make groups of words intelligible, and the omission of these marks may lead to misinterpretation or incomprehension by the reader. Only a slovenly or bad-mannered writer would omit all commas and full stops.

The correct position for a comma or full stop is level with the base of the middle zone of the previous letter. Higher placed marks may indicate enthusiasm, while lower placed ones suggest depression.

Any embellishment of punctuation is a desire for attention, perhaps a pseudo-artistic posing. This can be, for example, enclosing the full stop in a circle (except where this is done for copy editing purposes), enlarging commas, or emphasizing exclamation marks by their number, size or boldness.

A common fault is the use of excessive punctuation. This can take the form of a comma every three or four words, of an exclamation mark (or two) at the end of almost every sentence, and of frequent underlinings for emphasis. Such marks suggest a vain and snobbish writer who is fussy and self-opinionated but who is also worried about not being understood.

The use of punctuation may vary during the course of a sample of writing, indicating a mood change (perhaps brought on by the subject-matter involved.

Excessive punctuation is the mark of a pedantic and fussy writer (left and right).

Loops
Fullness and leanness

This is a different area of analysis from the width of letters, though one that is easily confused. Here we are concerned with the fullness or otherwise of loops.

If letters are of more than copybook fullness they are said to be full. This is most easily recognized in upper zone and lower zone loops, though it may also occur in the middle zone. The important thing here is to compare the degrees of fullness in the three zones. Where the same degree of fullness occurs throughout the zones it is generally regarded as a good sign. Only when it is restricted to one or two zones (particularly to the upper or lower zones) it is connected with any negative elements.

A full middle zone indicates a realistic, warm-hearted person, sociable and genial, though perhaps rather an individualist. But when only the middle zone is full (known as an artificial fullness) there is a suggestion of daydreaming and a lack of clear thought and an inability to respond emotionally.

A full upper zone suggests a realistic and constructive person and quite possibly a creative mind. But if only the upper zone is full there is a tendency towards fantasizing, daydreaming and over-enthusiasm, coupled with a lack of realism, concentration and self-criticism.

Full upper zone

Lower loops

sitting

writing

rmingham

going

engrossed

hunti

hay d

although

Yours

Truncated loop. The sudden stopping of the upward stroke reveals inhibitions; this indicates a cautious and possibly frigid person.

Small circle. This symbolizes the closed-off nature of the person involved, a self-contained isolationist.

Circle with stroke outwards. A loner who really wants self-assurance and security from association with others.

Filled loop. A very sensual person; possibly artistic.

Very short loop. Somebody lacking sexual drive, or else someone inexperienced with sex and suppressing the problem.

Leftward loop in rightward writing. If the writing pressure is light it suggests physical infirmity or a lack of energy; with heavy pressure it means problems with sex.

Loop ends in a strong downward stroke. Aggressive potential, particularly in sexual matters.

Very long loop. Indecisiveness through exhaustion.

Long full loop. This indicates a generous and emotional extrovert who is sexually impulsive, especially if the loop is made with heavy pressure; note that full loops to the left of the stem suggest backward-looking people while full loops to the right suggest forward-looking people.

Very large open loop. An extrovert with an excessive interest in material wealth.

Triangle with horizonal base. Obsessive interest in material wealth.

G or y loop with talon. A grasping or covetous person, unreasonable in small things.

G loop full, cutting through letter. A warm but self-effacing person.

Double loop. An individualist; perhaps a poseur; perhaps even neurotic.

Upper loops

The range of upper loops is smaller and has no relation to the writer's sexual problems or interest in material wealth.

Shortened loop. A self-effacing person, perhaps lacking originality.

Small high loop. An inhibited person, narrow-minded.

Very narrow loop. Suggests repressions.

Shaky loop. A person who lacks energy through age or infirmity, or somebody with mental problems.

Flattened loop. Obstinacy or aggression.

Leftward curving open loop. Very selfish attitude.

d your

but up

young

following Saturday

apologies

boy

and

leaving

book-hunting

lt, light

this

deemed

From top to bottom: full lower zone; lean upper zone; lean middle zone; lean lower zone.

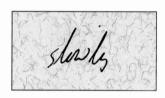

In the upper zone, covering strokes signify secretiveness about the writer's attitudes and outlook.

If it is the lower zone which is full, this means a sensual person, with strong instincts and sexual desires. But if only the lower zone is full, the sexual desires will be unrealistic or over-emphasized.

Leanness can be seen in any zone, though once again it is easier to spot in the upper and lower zones. It is defined as having loops less full than the copybook style.

A lean style indicates a rational, clear-thinking person, objective and with good business acumen. On the other hand, such people may well lack emotional warmth, may lack imagination, may have a low sex drive, and may harbour deep feelings of guilt and anxiety.

Upper and lower loops

These come in all kinds of shapes, not just full or lean. Upper and lower loops analysed separately are, lower loops first. Once again, beware of drawing solid conclusions from a single, small factor, such as loops; many people use a variety of loops depending upon the letter being written, whether it is the last letter of the word and the speed at which they are writing.

Covering strokes

These occur (most often in narrow or lean writing) where a second stroke in the construction of a letter covers or partly covers the first. The presence of these is supposed to indicate a very inhibited writer who feels the need to conceal something from other people. In order to analyse them, the zone and the connection type of the writing are important.

The person who uses covering strokes in the upper zone (the loop of the lower-case d, h and l, etc.) is generally secretive over plans and ideas. If it is the middle zone, the person is secretive about feelings and everyday situations, and is likely to be shy. And if it is the lower zone, the secretiveness is over sexual matters.

Where arcade connections are used, there is supposed to be frequent lying, shyness and restraint. If the connections are angular, there will be insincerity and trickery. If garland, shyness and emotional inhibition will be present; and if thread, there is an unwillingness to be committed to anything.

Numbers

Although we have less need to write numerals down than previously (having calculating machines instead of adding columns of figures by hand, print-outs instead of written bills, and credit cards instead of cheques), some aspects of personality show themselves when we do.

In general, the writer of simple, smooth, unambiguous numerals that are consistent, displays himself or herself as being competent, reliable and honest with a serious attitude towards material values, someone who is a responsible, careful user of money.

If the figures are small and neat this suggests somebody who has an analytical mind and who may regularly write figures, such as an accountant.

When the figures are poorly written, rather indistinct and ambiguous, the person may either be incompetent with numbers (unable to manage money), or perhaps dishonest (hoping that the numbers will be mistaken to his or her benefit), or perhaps just slovenly. In any case, such a person should not be in charge of handling money.

Heavy pressure on its own or combined with retouched figures suggests a person who is uncertain or anxious (or even neurotic) about money matters (or about material worth in general). This is most easily seen if the money figures have been retouched but other figures (the date, for example) have not.

It is worth comparing a person's ordinary numeral size (as in a letter) with numeral size on a cheque or when money is being denoted – often the money numerals will be larger, suggesting an unnatural concern with material values.

Where the numbers are decorated or embellished, suspect the writer of being artistic with little grasp of figures or monetary worth, even though the writer may be practical in other respects.

An exception is an embellished 7 with a cross stroke (7), which may be either the standard French form or an affectation.

Simple and clear numbers

Poorly formed and indistinct numbers

Small and neat numbers

Decorated numbers

Elaboration and simplification

Flourishes and embellishments are a feature of some people's writing. There is not necessarily anything wrong with this, so long as it is consistent and legible.

Undoubtedly, the clearest type of writing is that which omits all unnecessary strokes, achieving great simplicity. This is fine so long as it does not omit any important strokes and so long as it remains clearly legible. It demonstrates a mature, objective person with good judgement, intellectual faculties, clear thought and an economic attitude. Unless, that is, it becomes too cryptic, showing neglect, unreliability, a lack of consideration and a lack of sincerity.

A script which is of a good form level (generally neat, consistent and legible) is thought of as being enhanced or enriched by a few flourishes, but it is a difficult job to differentiate between enhancement and vulgarity. Perhaps this is always a subjective matter.

A copybook style looks neat and legible, but it may indicate a lack of character, and a lack of originality or creativity or emotion in its writer.

Vulgar ostentation through the addition of flourishes indicates poor taste, pedantic views, vanity, pomposity, conceitedness, over-compensation for an inferiority complex, pretension, and a need to be accepted by others.

A simple, easily legible style

A cryptic, semi-elaborate style

An elaborate, flamboyant style

Cary Grant

Here is an extreme example of an actor whose very large and showy writing, especially the capitals, make the graphologist think of him as self-centred, arrogant and conceited, with poor taste. Some of this exaggeration may be compensation for a lack of self-confidence, or even an artificial style adopted as an attention-grabber on the instructions of an agent.

In fact, setting the capitals aside, the rest of the writing is fluent and generally of good form with garland connections (tolerant, outgoing). Only the lack of lower loops – the straight stem of the y in two cases – has a negative meaning, that of fault-finding.

Capital letters

When considering capitals you must look at their relative size and at their general shape and degree of simplicity or ornamentation. Capitals should be just twice the height of middle zone letters; otherwise they are classed as large or small. The relationship here is with the writer's ego. The shape, on the other hand, can give an indication of self-consciousness, taste and creativity.

Large capital letters are often met with, especially in the first capital of a piece of writing. They tend to be not only more than twice the height of the middle zone but much wider than lower-case letters. They indicate a writer seeking status (an ambitious person) or enjoying his or her current feelings of high status. The person is self-regarding, proud and probably a dreamer.

When the capital is also particularly broad it suggests a show-off who may be arrogant, over-ambitious, lacking in self-criticism or judgement. But the person will probably also be self-reliant, imaginative and outgoing.

Large and ornate capitals suggest crudity, lack of taste and a pompous nature; perhaps also generosity and certainly ostentation.

A long, thin, narrow capital can indicate slyness, an unwillingness to acknowledge weaknesses, and the presence of introversion and inhibitions. On the positive side, it means ambition, thrift and a sensitive nature.

Large capital

Ornate capital

Broad capital

Long, narrow capital

Small capital

Separate capital

Wrongly positioned capital

Odd capital

Where the capitals are small it suggests an unassuming, shy person with a lack of self-confidence, or perhaps just an intellectual who prefers to remain in the background. The same may be said of those who employ a lower-case style of capital.

If the capitals are joined up to following letters it indicates fluency of thought, all details being worked out in advance, and good planning skills.

If the capitals stand on their own, away from the rest of the word, it can mean that the writer plays hunches, uses intuition and may be inspired at times.

Where capitals appear normal-sized but too narrow, we find a careful, suspicious individual who is used to disappointment and self-restraint.

Whenever capitals have been touched up or amended to make them appear taller, the person is anxious and has a desire for improvement.

Capitals sometimes appear in the wrong place – even inside words. Or there may just be too many capitalized words. This may indicate a person who gives greater than necessary importance to small things, someone who overreacts, is under emotional pressure, is unintelligent, is unsettled, or is lying.

Very simple capitals (printed rather than written) suggest literary ability and possible artistic skill. They indicate a cultured, reliable person.

Some people use odd capitals – ornate but strange or humorous – which indicate an open, friendly, co-operative type.

When there an abnormally large gap before and after the I, it indicates feelings of being isolated and comfort derived from privacy. When the gap is distinctly shorter after than before, the person is afraid of solitude.

Where the I is much taller than the other letters there is a feeling of superiority, especially in intelligence and intellect. Perhaps this is over-compensation for an inferiority complex.

A large variation of capital I forms in one sample suggests a flexible but unpredictable person.

A much smaller than expected I indicates a lack of confidence. Heavy pressure shows strain, tension and maybe compulsive behaviour. Light pressure means inhibitions, feelings of inferiority and a very submissive personality.

Capital connected to following letter

Touched-up capital

Printed capital

Capital I

Here we must differentiate between the ordinary capital I and the personal pronoun; it is the latter which gives a good indication of the writer's ego. It should be examined for its size, slant, fullness, general form, pressure and spacing.

A solitary, simple downstroke. The writer has no affectations; there is a straightforward approach to life; this is a natural, probably cultured person.

A simple stroke; bottom curves to right. Eagerness to embrace the future.

A simple stroke amended or thickened by extra strokes. A lack of confidence; some anxiety or even neurosis.

With serifs. A cultured, businesslike person, confident, independent, practical and constructive.

With serifs, shaky. Illness affecting enthusiasm and confidence.

Small instead of capital. Lack of self-esteem.

A simple stroke with a bottom curve to the left. A controlled and economical person, lacking surface emotions.

A writing-type letter with a straight finish. Independent.

Same as last, with an open top. Talkative and self-assured.

Starting at the base. A rebellious nature.

Copybook. Self-esteem and confidence.

Compressed. Narrow-minded.

Very wide. An extrovert, perhaps mother-influenced.

Very wide lower loop. An extrovert with sexual fantasies.

Angled top, long sharp base. Aggressive, self-righteous.

Hesitant. Uncommitted, self-defeating; elderly/infirm.

Two parts. Traumatized, perhaps only temporarily.

Open. Communicative, co-operative.

Intro from right. Humorous, talkative.

Loop up into upper zone. Contemplative type.

Open, very large loop. Vain.

Open, huge loop. Megalomaniac.

Scrolled. Greed.

Old-fashioned. Restrained, cautious, old-fashioned.

Very angular. Critical, hostile; the angular base means feelings of resentment and disappointment.

Complex. Great feelings of pride and self-worth; often compensating for an inferiority complex.

Different slant from normal writing. An individualist who has secret obsessions.

A loop resembling a lower-case L. A casual statement of individuality.

Very rightward slant. A need for personal contact; if in a leftward script it means great shyness and fear of failure.

i-dots and
t-bars

Because the way in which people dot their i and cross
their t is easy to spot and is capable of huge variation,
these are commonly held up as significant aspects of
one's writing style. In fact, while they can be used to
confirm a personality analysis, they should not be over-
emphasized or analysed in isolation. A close examination
of any fairly long handwriting sample may show a considerable variation in i-dots and t-bars; up to four or five
different versions (of each) might well be found. The
reasons for this are different letters following the i or t,
and changes in mood or speed – and this is a perfectly
normal range of variation.

The i-dot

Taking the i-dot first, the factors governing its analysis
are:

(a)   Its horizontal relationship to the downstroke.
(b)   Its shape.
(c)   Its connection (if any) to other letters.
(d)   Its vertical position.

Here is a selection of the more common forms in a very
large range, with their interpretations.

I-dot variations

Missing dot. This suggests a lazy or forgetful person, though if the rest of the sample is careful it may show resourcefulness.

Perfectly placed. Shows a careful, precise person who plans ahead; not usually a fast writer; may be a rather slow, methodical person, unused to writing.

To the right. Fast-moving writing and thoughts; impatience, impulsiveness, enthusiasm.

To the left. Caution; probably a slow writer, introverted and hesitant.

Weak dot. Lack of self-confidence; lack of vitality.

Heavy dot. Depression, subservience.

Arrowhead open to the right. The sign of an alert mind; good speed and observation.

Arrowhead open to the left. Sharp-tongued and sarcastic; again, good observation.

Accent. A critical mind, inclined towards irritability.

Grave accent. Slap-dash attitude to life.

Circle. A slow writer, perhaps with an artistic temperament; maybe an immature person or a poseur.

Heavy oblong. Great passion.

Horizontal dash. A hypersensitive individual.

Vertical dash. Narrow-minded, petty.

Not connected to the next letter. A mature and intelligent person who thinks and writes rapidly; good co-ordination.

High to the right. An outgoing attitude; extroversion and good humour.

Low. A practical, realistic and down-to-earth person.

Chris Evert Lloyd

Playing tennis and winning at the highest level is, of course, part of the entertainment industry. In order to succeed you must show off. The very large signature here, with its exceptionally tall and broad capitals, shows a big ego, with feelings of self-importance and self-confidence. The single paraph emphasizes these characteristics.

This is a simple and easily read signature, written by a person who is generally considerate and wants to be understood. The full name suggests a need for clarity (though, of course, it also shows that she was proud enough of being married to John Lloyd to want to add his name to hers even for professional purposes, but didn't want to drop the well-known Evert name).

There is strong emotion in the big loops, as well as creativity. Indeed, the capacity for emotion, combined with sensitivity, is emphasized by the lightness of touch. The whole signature has a good flow, with plenty of vitality, indicating a clear and fast thinker.

Ingrid Bergman

Not only is it unusual for an actress to use her real name, but it is very uncommon to find thread connections and a scarcely larger than average signature. The thread connections mark her out as a rebel with a dislike of authority and rules. There may be some insecurity here, too.

The large capitals denote ambition. The simple signature, completely lacking in flourishes or paraphs, shows no ego problem and a refreshing simplicity of outlook. The way in which the two words of the signature become smaller towards their ends suggest a person who is shy and cautious to the point of suspicion.

The t-bar

In general, t-bars indicate leadership qualities, but again beware of reading too much into a sample on its own; there is bound to be some variation and the analysis should be used to confirm other findings, not to stand alone. Any heavy strokes will tend to be part of heavy, aggressive writing, using angular connections and fast

T-bar variations

 No bar. Absent-minded or perhaps rebellious; perhaps an ineffectual person.

 To the left. Cautious, indecisive, lacking self-confidence, perhaps depressed.

 Touching to the left. Self-conscious; fear of social contact.

Short bar. Timidity; a lack of drive and enthusiasm.

Long bar. Ambitious, confident; a leader.

 Light bar. Sensitive, easily influenced, retiring.

 Heavy bar. Selfish, determined and domineering.

Balanced on stem. A leader with ambition and imagination.

 Hooked. Determined.

 Concave. Self-protective, repressed, irresponsible.

 Convex. Poor self-control, but imaginative and well-coordinated.

 Low bar. Depressed; little self-esteem; sulky.

 Wavy bar. Sense of fun.

 Knotted bar. Persistent, obstinate, thorough.

Curved rightward bar. A critical person; not always truthful.

speed. Note that while some graphologists feel that the slope of the bar is of little importance, others believe than an upward sloping bar is a guide to optimism and a downward sloping bar a warning of a hypercritical or domineering person.

Here is a selection of some of the more common types together with their meanings.

If lots of letters are joined by the t-bar (in a single stroke the length of the whole word), this denotes a quick, agile mind, often a quick writer, and a person who tends to be a good problem-solver.

Looped top of stem. Emotional, talkative.   *that*

Curlicue. Egotistic.   *cate*

Double bar. A neurotic person; a lack of self-assurance.   *Saturday*

Long detached to the right. A fantasist; indecisive.   *time*

Short detached to the right. A person who welcomes challenges and new ideas.   *assorted*

Short attached to the right. A precise person who sticks to the rules. If this is a frequent usage it suggests a person unused to writing.   *it*

Star-shaped. Sensitive to criticism; lacking self-assurance.   *it*

Long triangular stroke. Potential for aggression; objects to interference.   *that*

Copybook. Perhaps unused to writing; perhaps vain, emotional and insecure.   *t*

Upside-down. Liable to invert facts, too.   *extrovert.*

Single-stroke stem and loop. Over-independent; perhaps fanatical or aggressive.   *that*

Almost like an S. Quick-thinking, enthusiastic.   *christmas*

Straight stem with a bottom loop. Unemotional, tightly controlled.   *thes*

Single curve incorporating bar and stem. Vague, indecisive.   *thank*

Some variation of t-bars within a sample is only to be expected, but if there is a great mixture (particularly within one paragraph or line) it suggests a changeable, emotional mind that is insecure and never satisfied.

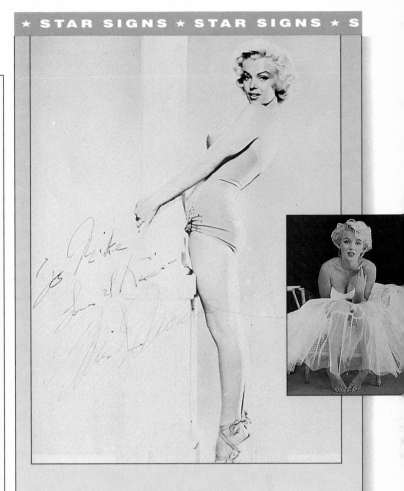

Marilyn Monroe

This was the stage name used by Norma Jean Baker, who committed suicide in 1962 at the age of 36. Its strangest feature is the very light pressure, indicating shyness, some introversion and perhaps extreme sensitivity. There is a lack of self-confidence here, in the very large and flowery capitals and in that extremely long flourish from the e of Monroe.

The written message is, by comparison, heavier, more variable and much poorer in form, with a tiny middle zone, suggesting that she might have been tense writing something unfamiliar for someone unfamiliar. It also bears signs of haste and, like the signature, is meant to catch the eye. The optimism of its angle means that she was feeling good when she wrote it.

The fact that the Marilyn is almost illegible probably didn't matter; her signature was known to many. Only the way in which the arms of the k cut its stem shows that she might have been resentful about anything.

Signatures

Your signature is even more significant than the way your write a capital I in judging how you want to be seen by the world at large. You are, in effect, saying "this is me" in the way you sign your name. Features such as size relative to your normal writing, relative sizes of letters within the signature, legibility, slant, direction and any embellishments are all important factors in the analysis.

But a signature on its own provides insufficient material for a graphologist to use in order to come up with a reliable assessment of personality.

The basic structure of people's signatures tends to become standardized during the later teens or early twenties, as adulthood beckons. It remains more or less the same for forty or fifty years at least, until old age or infirmity introduces hesitation and unsteadiness. At the same time, one's general style of writing may change, leaving great differences between the signature and any other words.

Of course, signatures, too, may be changed. A woman will often take her husband's surname on marriage and will need to adjust to the different signature. A person who becomes famous may deliberately cultivate a more expansive signature to fit in with their image, or may be forced to create a signature if their public name differs

Larger first name

Larger second name

Initials in place of forenames

Illegible (simple)

Illegible (complex)

from their real one. Examples here are actors, pop stars, sports personalities and authors. In addition, some people who are often asked for their autograph develop a compressed or simplified signature in order to save time and effort. Thus it is quite common for personalities to have two different signatures – one for private purposes and another for their adoring public.

One of the easiest points to spot is a signature's size relative to other words. A large signature denotes a person who thinks of himself or herself as important and wants others to think the same. There is pride showing here, perhaps forcefulness and great self-esteem, but sometimes also compensation for a lack of self-confidence. Certainly it represents a desire for betterment.

Where the signature is smaller than other words the person is trying to appear modest. This may be the result of a mild, self-deprecating personality; it may be a defence mechanism; it may show a genuine lack of self-esteem; or it may be a pose.

A signature where the letters are of comparable size to that individual's normal writing shows a sincere, modest and unpretentious person who is not concerned with self-image and is very objective about his or her own good and bad points. There may be a tendency towards complacency.

Where the first name is emphasized by larger writing than for the surname, this may indicate that the person prefers informality (first name terms), was happiest in childhood (when that first name was perhaps more used), or, in the case of a married woman, was happier before marriage, using her maiden name, or even that the person prefers the first name or dislikes the surname for the same reason. A much enlarged or embellished first name is a mark of self-love.

On the other hand, if the surname is over-emphasized it is most probably for reasons of prestige.

What form of your name should you sign? Although there may be good individual reasons for a person using their name in full, in a signature this can indicate snobbishness. (However, it may be for the purpose of better identification if it is a common surname.) When the initials only are used, this can suggest stand-offishness or a dislike of familiarity.

Another reason for signatures differing from other writing is that they are usually written faster because the writer will swing into a familiar pattern without needing to think. Only the most painstaking or pedantic of people (perhaps bank-managers or lawyers, who recognize the importance of a signature) may sign more slowly than they write.

For a similar reason – fast writing – many signatures are illegible. Quite a large proportion of these are of a wavy line or thread shape. This suggests a secretive writer, an uncaring writer or a hasty and unthinking writer. It is certainly bad manners to cultivate an illegible signature. When a signature is illegible but complex it might well indicate an excessive vanity, coupled with stand-offishness.

Many signatures consist not only of the writer's name but also of flourishes, underlinings or dots.

Where the last letter of the surname is continued in a flourish towards the right (more or less horizontally) this suggests a writer lacking in self-confidence. If the continuation curves gently upwards, generosity is signified, but if it goes up at a sharp angle this is considered a mark of aggression. If that last letter is extended in a vigorous curving movement this may be a sign of a forceful personality, but if the flourish becomes too ornate or deliberate it is the mark of somebody who wants to look and feel important, in other words somebody who feels inferior.

In some signatures the flourish cuts back through the name, crossing it out, suggesting a great lack of self-confidence, a person whose self-esteem is low. This may be a temporary feature, indicating that the person needs help with psychological problems. If the signature is circled or boxed in, the writer feels isolated from the world (or wants to avoid contact with others); either way, there is some serious ego problem. If any of these indications are accompanied by lines dipping towards the right, by breaks in words, by very small or light pressure handwriting, or by a strong leftward slant, the writer should probably be seeking help.

Any piece of underlining or partial underlining is technically known as a paraph. Anything of this kind is unconscious compensation for feelings of inferiority (in particular, the writer feels inferior to the person being written to and adds the paraph as a defence mechanism). The actual paraph is being used to emphasize the writer's name (or part of it) in an attempt to feel better (to improve the condition of the ego). A single line of normal pressure emphasizes the ego. A single heavy line shows an aggressive, assertive personality. A long rising line denotes ambition. A short line can mean a weaker personality, easily impressed by others; if this paraph is just under the first name it can mean an appeal for informality (or for that particular form of the first name to be used); if it is just under the surname it suggests the reverse.

A double line (forward and back) represents an attempt at the dramatic, though several of them suggests an overbearing, uncompromising nature, while a heavy double line (two parallel lines) means a determined but selfish person. The line with hooks at either end is a cry for recognition. If the line is very ornate, with much scrolling, suspect an affectedly artistic poseur – often

Curved flourish

Ornate flourish

Circled signature

Short paraph

Long, rising paraph

with poor taste. When there are lines above and below the signature, the writer is probably a shy and lonely person, distrustful of others and very unsure of himself or herself.

Dots are often an integral part of the signature. A concluding dot indicates that the writer thinks of his or her name as the final thing. This will probably be a cautious, prudent person who insists on having the last word. If the dot becomes a colon, the writer is feeling the intention to write more and is unsure whether or not to do so. A dot before the signature or an unnecessary dot during it suggests that the writer has paused, perhaps due to some inhibition or behavioural problem (unless for reason of old age or infirmity).

The positioning of the signature beneath a piece of writing is meant to be important. A central signature indicates modesty and caution. To the left means a shy and retiring person, while to the right means an active, impatient individual. When the signature is close to the other writing, the writer is indicating a close bond with the content or with the recipient, or both. And if the signature is placed very low, with a wide gap, this is an attempt to distance himself or herself from the text. The general form level of the signature is worth considering. Some signatures are beautiful constructions which may reflect a controlled artistry or, if exaggerated, may suggest a show-off. A rising signature means an optimistic mood and a falling signature a pessimistic mood – but only at the time of signing.

The slant of a signature is not always the same as that of the person's normal writing. A rightward script with a leftward signature indicates the presence of barriers – the writer is applying control to the normal writing and only the signature is spontaneous. Or it might be that the signature has been leftward since adolescence, when the writing was also leftward. A leftward script with a rightward signature is the sign of a shy person, perhaps rather cold towards others, who is trying to appear outgoing for professional reasons. An upright script with a rightward signature suggests an attempt at warmth by an introverted person. An upright signature with a rightward script suggests a warm person trying to appear cool and businesslike for professional reasons.

With concluding dot

Signature close to piece of writing

Rising

Falling

Writing and signature of different slants

A signature's size in relation to the writer's normal writing indicates the state of the ego. A very large signature may be a type of boastfulness or exhibitionism, as is a very idiosyncratic signature (though both may be a cover for a lack of confidence). A very small signature is a surer pointer to confidence problems.

Colours of ink, paper and envelopes

What does it mean when somebody writes you letters in green ink or red ink? And why are they using pale mauve writing-paper?

The answer is that there may or may not be some psychological significance in the ink and paper colours. It is only worth trying to analyse these if you are sure that the colour was a deliberate choice, and is regularly bought and used by that person.

It is all too easy to pick up a pen almost at random and scribble a note without there being any meaning to the ink colour – even if it is rather unusual. Only when the colour is known to be consistently used may it be significant.

Inks

Blue

So many people these days use a ball-point with a pale blue refill that it would be foolish to try to draw any conclusions. Do they all use pale blue only because it is so readily available, or is it so readily available because it is genuinely the first choice of most people?

Where a fountain-pen and ink are used, again blue is common. Here a more intense blue is chosen because it is pleasant, perhaps even uplifting, without being at all unusual.

Royal blue ink is supposed to be a colour used often by women because it stresses their femininity, suggesting affection, understanding and sociability.

Blue-black ink is a no-nonsense shade often used by men and by people in business and commerce. It is regarded as being very conventional.

Black

Formerly the standard in business, this has become the preserve of the writer who is (or who would like to be considered) bold, forceful and serious. Used with a broad nibbed pen it indicates the ambitious businessman, designer or student. When used with a thinner nib, it suggests an artistic personality, still serious though possibly rebellious and depressed. Generally, black denotes a need to be clearly understood.

Brown

Most black ink goes brown with age, so any old handwriting samples in brown will have begun life as black.

Where brown ink is employed it is a deliberate statement, usually by an artistic person who wants to be different, to stand out, but who still needs the security of a dark and non-flashy colour. It is thought to have the look of authority about it.

Red

Because it stands out, red ink is used by the person who really wants to be different, who wants to shock others. Red is associated with danger, excitement, anger and sex. Sometimes the person who writes in red will be trying to give undue weight or emphasis to their words. Look out for red ink coupled with great pressure and perhaps angular connections, all pointing towards an angry writer. On the other hand, there is a possibility that the writer will be a professional who often uses red (a teacher, for example) or a rather pompous or pedantic person. Beware of deducing too much from the use of this colour of ink and look for other signs.

Green

Another colour which stands out (as much for its unusualness as for its shade), green is also used by the individualistic writer who wants his or her words to become more important than they are. There are difficulties in interpretation here, too, because it may be used by a person who is young and/or artistic or who just wants to show off, or it may be the mark of a strong-minded and flexible person. On the other hand, it may be used for its ecological or political connotations. Other evidence is needed before one can draw firm conclusions.

Turquoise

Turquoise is considered to be a woman's colour. It is bright and different, with suggestions of an artistic nature, or perhaps just artistic pretensions.

Violet

Thought to be trendy and slightly camp, this has traditionally been used by those with theatrical connections. It has often turned up in conjunction with brightly coloured paper, revealing the writer as somebody with bad taste and emotional immaturity who has a need for recognition.

Glitter

Various shiny and metallic inks are available, of which gold and silver are the most commonly used. They are not the most practical of writing substances and tend to be expensive, so they are used purely for show by those with artistic pretensions (except for a limited number of legitimate artistic or calligraphic purposes). The theatricality of this suggests a person who uses fantasy to escape from reality.

Colour variation

Harsh words have been used by some graphologists to describe anyone who dares to employ more than one colour of ink within a sample of writing (for underlining, or for the first letter of each sentence, or perhaps for alternate paragraphs). While there is a certain playfulness or childishness in such behaviour, it does not indicate any serious mental disorder. And what about those medieval monks who spent their lives doing it?

Coloured paper

Writing-paper seems to be such a common present that, even where a person uses a particular shade regularly, it is dangerous to assume that it represents their personality.

The writer who is of good taste and not ostentatious will most often choose white, cream or a pale blue. Pale pink is regarded as very feminine. In fact, the brighter and more unusual paper colours are almost always used by women rather than men, and are associated with artistic or romantic personalities, sometimes with a degree of pretension.

Envelopes

To continue the colour theme, coloured envelopes may be thought to carry the same personality connotations as coloured writing-paper, though cards of all kinds are often sold these days with bright envelopes (red or green in particular) over which the writer has no control. Because most envelopes are white or brown, the envelope colour is not the most fruitful of areas for personality analysis.

However, the manner of addressing the envelope, in particular the positioning of the address, is a trait much studied by graphologists.

The ideal is supposed to be a central placing, in clearly legible writing, with each line beginning from the same

A step design points to an instinctive distrust of people and the need to take time to establish relationships.

Block design favoured by the conventional, considerate writer.

With the address at the top, the writer is ignoring the realities of life and falling prey to fantasies.

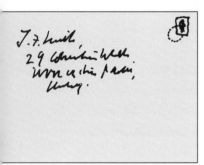

By contrast, with the address at the bottom, material concerns predominate as does a pessimistic outlook on life.

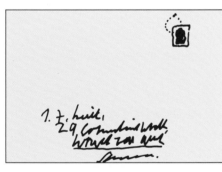

The showman, always keen to attract attention, makes an exhibition of any envelope.

The extrovert pushes his address to the right; the opposite applies to the introvert.

(imaginary) vertical margin, and with no underlining or confusing messages. All of this suggests a clear-thinking and well-organized person who plans, is considerate, is neat and is not over-fussy.

If the lines of the address are successively stepped this may display caution and a distrust of people, or it may just be that the writer habitually uses what was a former business practice.

Where the name and address are placed high up, using only the top half of the envelope, this indicates immaturity (children address envelopes this way), carelessness, a lack of thought and a dreamy, fantasizing attitude towards life.

A very low positioning suggests anxiety and pessimism, but possibly also great concern with material things.

A placement to the right of the envelope is meant to reflect the extrovert, while a placement to the left reflects the introvert, except that a low left placement may simply be a careful and well-organized attempt to leave plenty of room for stamps and franking marks.

Where the address is large and/or spaced out, occupying most of the envelope, the writer is probably an exhibitionist – a person with a larger-than-life personality who loves to be at the centre of events. If the writing is ornate this will just confirm that person's vain and pretentious nature.

Any underlining (except where it is a national convention to emphasize some element of the address) suggests a fussy, pedantic person who worries about small things and lacks good judgement. The same may be said of anyone who writes "Confidential" or "Urgent" on the front of the envelope; such messages and underlinings often confuse rather than help.

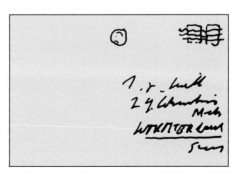

Signs of stress and tension

Stress and tension

All of us are subject to stress in our lives. Often we do not realize when the stress burden, instead of merely stimulating us to try harder, is affecting our well-being.

One way in which graphological analysis can help us all is in identifying when stress has become too great. It can even suggest which area of life is primarily responsible for the intolerable stress, allowing something to be done before one's health is seriously affected.

This is an area of graphology with clear benefit, which you can try out on yourself or on family and friends.

Bear in mind the possibility that some of these "signs of stress" may be natural elements in a writing style, so the presence of several signs is needed for a diagnosis of excess stress.

Here are the major signs, placed in approximate order of ease of recognition:

(a)   The left-hand margin is narrow, but the right-hand margin is wide.

(b)   Lines are lower towards the right, either sloping or tilting.

(c)   There is considerable underlining of words.

(d)   The whole writing sample has a generally irregular appearance.

(e)   Words are widely spaced, but letters are crammed closely together.

(f)   The signature is smaller than usual, smaller than the normal writing, and may be underlined.

(g)   The slant varies – in particular, moving more towards the left.

(h)   There is much evidence of a disturbed rhythm, including gaps in the middle of words, letters missing, letters touched up or overwritten, and varying pressure.

(i)   Capitals tend to be large.

(j)   Letters tend to be small, but variable in size.

(k)   Letters tend to be narrow, with covering strokes.

(l)   While letters are carefully formed, this has been done with slow and deliberate strokes, using two or more strokes where one would have sufficed, and with some evidence of an unsteady hand.

(m)   The base line is not constant.

(n)   Pressure is heavy in one or more zones, with noticeably heavy starting strokes.

(o)   The middle zone tends to be smaller than normal, and the upper zone taller and narrower.

(p)   There may be more punctuation than normal.

(q)   Dots may be visible where the pen has been rested between words or letters while thinking (feel the other side of the paper).

Doodles

As we have seen, unconscious stress often bubbles to the surface in handwriting, through sudden changes of slant, spacing, margins and other oddities. We can discover other hidden traits – as well as our secret fears and desires – through the examination of doodles. These relaxing and playful jottings are designs or pictures produced by parts of our minds without conscious control. They are said to be a reversion to the childish scribblings which were our first attempts at drawing.

Many people find that doodling helps them to relieve tension or anxiety. It is often done while one is waiting, or during a meeting or a lecture while the conscious mind is concentrating on something else. The doodler may even be working his or her way through a problem of some kind.

Doodles take many forms, and may be pictures, cartoons or patterns, in lines, blobs or dots. Quite often a doodle will be repeated by the same person, at intervals, over many years.

Some people never doodle. They tend to be tightly controlled individuals who are precise and direct in their dealings with others.

(1)   A chaotic pattern of short strokes in the form of crosses means inner conflict, perhaps a battle against restrictions of some sort. Or it may signify an attempt to relax after an actual conflict, such as a quarrel. There is anger in the crosses, even though the strokes were done with light pressure.

(2)   Cones drawn in series like this are undoubtedly phallic symbols. The looseness of the drawing suggests a mood of relaxation.

(3)   Groups of flower heads are supposed to be a phallic symbol. These are obviously very quickly done, with swift circular strokes and little concern for accuracy or outline. Even the number of petals varies from five to seven. A casual and relaxed attitude is indicated.

(4)   The extreme delicacy of these leaf shapes suggests concentration and the development of ideas. The adjacent piece of curved frame (against the edge of the sheet of paper) further suggests development; the way in which it has been shaded is indicative of a systematic mind.

(5)   Circular designs may refer to breasts or to motherhood, though this one is more probably an expression of the completeness of a circle (despite its bitty appearance).

(6)   An open curve refers either to the emotions (especially if the lines are heavy) or to feelings of puzzlement and a lack of certainty, so that the curve may be based upon a question mark.

(7)   The angular framework, with lots of lines crossing, indicates anger or resentment which is only just being controlled.

(8)   A feather stands for femininity. It is quite common for women to produce such shapes unconsciously stating their femininity.

(9)   Whether you see it as a hollow tube or a rolling pin, this is probably a phallic symbol, drawn with enough artistry to suggest great powers of concentration and neatness.

(10)   There is a logical mind at work here, indicated by the linked whorls and circles. Suggestions of anxiety are present, too, especially in the heavy pressure and the crossing lines.

(11)   Geometrical or architectural shapes produced with heavy strokes are a reaction to everyday routine. There is a feeling of being trapped expressed here. The perspective lines (reaching into the future) suggest a bleak expectation.

(12)   Any heavily shaded shapes are symptomatic of frustration or anger.

It is worth noting that a shrunken middle zone indicates a deflated ego, that an extended upper zone means too much fantasizing, and that a truncated lower zone suggests physical weakness or sexual repression.

Stimulus words

Even where there is no excessive stress on a person, he or she is very likely to write particular words in a different style. These are stimulus words. They trigger off emotional associations within the writer.

The words will often be the names of places or people (perhaps parents) connected with love or hate or shame in the writer's mind, though they may be references to sex or death.

How may the words be recognized? The answer is that they will stand out as being written differently, perhaps because they are more carefully written, even with strokes touched up, or maybe with a different slant to the rest of the sample. It may even be that the word will have been completely retraced, or that there will be a gap in the middle of it. Another approach is that the writer, instead of taking more care, will take less – will hurry through the word at greater speed, using a light pressure, both trying to get the word out of the way as quickly as possible and attempting to conceal it with the illegibility of a quick flourish. (This is clearly an unconscious activity.)

Note that when writers feel stressed, or when they are afraid of stimulus words occurring, they will sometimes change to a printed script. This can act as a barrier, since it is not subject to graphological analysis.

Phil Collins

The fast, expansive signature suggests an adaptable, enthusiastic and fast-thinking extrovert. He seems to be a logical thinker with a great fluency of thought. The extensive flourish at the end of the surname and the double paraph are attention-grabbing devices, as one would expect from a major star of pop/rock music.

Yet there are some indications of a slight lack of self-confidence, while the signature is not particularly large, or at least no larger than the other writing, so perhaps we have a sincere and modest person here, with no ego problem.

The missing letters in both names are more likely the result of haste than insincerity. The capital P, being so large, may suggest a desire for informality, though the narrow capital C is more of a negative point. A sense of fun is indicated by the drawing.

Two examples from the same piece of writing. At the stress words "insomnia" and "anorexic", the writing becomes slower, more rounded and approaches printed script, thereby signifying the writer's unconscious anxiety.

Reliability and unreliability

This is where graphology moves from being a bit of fun or a parlour game to being a scientific tool of personnel selection.

Is graphology scientific enough to be applied in this way? Does your handwriting really reveal how reliable or unreliable a person you are? Can there, in any case, be an absolute answer to a person's reliability or honesty? Is there any guarantee that even the most reliable of people will never make a crucial mistake? The line between honesty and dishonesty is still more difficult to draw – who can say that they have has never stolen a sheet of paper or a paperclip?

There are two ways of answering these knotty problems. One is to accept that graphology is used for these purposes, and has been so used over many years. A great many organizations in continental Europe have employed graphology in personnel selection for decades. In the US it is meant to be part of the selection procedure of the FBI and is coming to be used by more and more firms. In Britain it is more popular each year, with many freelance graphologists offering their services to large and small firms. Could all these organizations be mistaken? The other answer is that testing for reliability is the most difficult of all the tasks that the graphologist is called upon to perform.

In practice, the graphologist goes through the handwriting sample carefully, checking it against a large number of factors that are accepted as indicators of unreliability or dishonesty. If several factors occur (an absolute minimum of five, preferably at least seven or eight) then the subject of the analysis is branded as, for example, "unreliable, tending to be dishonest"; if a job application is involved, the candidate will probably be passed over. Analysis is not a simple procedure. It takes experience and professionalism to judge a person in this way and have confidence in your verdict.

Test yourself for reliability against these factors – but bear in mind the fact that most people have one or two bad tendencies in their handwriting, so any isolated signs can be ignored. Also, it will probably be uncertain to you whether certain factors occur in your handwriting or not; remember that it takes a professional to provide an accurate assessment.

(b) Poor form/illegibility

(j) Threads within words

(k) Incomplete letters

(k) Ambiguous letters

(p) Too many strokes per letter

(a) *Slow writing.* A mature and intelligent person should not be writing slowly, except perhaps due to illness or a language problem, unless something is being concealed.

(b) *Generally poor form level.* Varying pressure and slant suggest an unstable personality; if illegible this indicates at least an inconsiderate person, at worst an attempt to hide things.

(c) *A simple, copybook style.* This suggests immaturity or concealment; perhaps the writer is still a teenager.

(d) *A leftward slant.* Unreliability, untruthfulness.

(e) *Initial letters are enlarged.* An attempt to make a good impression.

(f) *Touching up of letters without improvements.* Nervousness, lack of self-confidence; an attempt to make reality match expectation.

(g) *Unnecessary dots.* These resting points suggest pauses due to uncertainty or strain.

(h) *Covering strokes.* Suggests something to hide.

(i) *Arcade connections.* Suggests unreliability and something to hide.

(j) *Threads within words.* Suggests an elusive or insincere person.

(k) *Incomplete or ambiguous letters.* An unwillingness to accept reality and an impolite disregard for other people.

(l) *Unnecessary embellishments.* An attempt at obscuring the issue or to cover up a lack of self-confidence.

(m) *Letters not closed at their bases.* A selfish and potentially rebellious person.

(n) *Signature illegible or very different from other writing.* Suggests disregard for others, intentional concealment, or a person with an ego problem.

(o) *Letters deleted or written in the wrong order.* A dislike of commitments (unless the writer is dyslexic).

(p) *Letters written with more strokes than necessary.* Nervous, unsure, under strain.

(q) *Hooks on letters.* A selfish person, especially where the hooks are leftward.

(r) *Sharks' teeth.* Secretiveness and deceit.

(s) *Important parts missing from letters.* A secretive person, concealing information, distracting attention.

(t) *Numerals unclear.* Suggests a misleading person.

(u) *A great mixture of connective forms.* A weak and vacillating person, easily led.

It is worth noting that the best test for reliability (rather than unreliability) is to check on consistency. A really consistent writer in terms of slant, spacings and style, who also writes clearly and fairly quickly, is likely to be extremely reliable.

★ STAR SIGNS ★ STAR SIGNS ★ S

Jimi Hendrix

This was the stage form of his name used by James Marshall Hendrix, perhaps the greatest rock guitarist, who died in 1970 at the age of 29, under the influence of drugs.

His large signature, full of flourishes, shows that he thought of himself as important and needed attention; it may have covered up a lack of self-confidence. The extremely long T-bar is a very assertive factor. The equally long J-bar is a flaunting stroke, an attention-grabber, but it also serves to cover up the rest of the signature, concealing the individual. The strong downward plunge of the H upright suggests vigour and determination.

A noteworthy factor is the way in which the strokes seem to have been painted rather than written, indicating a warm, emotional person with strong artistic feelings and plenty of ideas. The careful message has been slowly written in mostly unconnected strokes (visual acuity and a great sense of artistic balance here), while the signature has been scribbled by comparison, probably due to haste and simple neglect. There is considerable optimism shown by the smile line of the H-bar and the rising lines of writing.

Forgery

It is extremely difficult to forge another person's signature or style of writing with any accuracy. What one person does automatically can only be reproduced imperfectly by someone else – and then only at a slower speed, so that the rhythm of the original is lost. For this reason, a slow copybook style of writing is probably the easiest to forge successfully.

Forgers tend not to be graphologists. They look at the most noticeable points of their victim's writing and try to imitate those. These noticeable points include capital letters, the beginnings of words, and the loops of the upper and lower zones. It may be that the forger will make a good job of all of these, but at the same time will ignore the middle zone and will probably get the other ingredients wrong, in particular the endings of words.

Although our handwriting varies from one sample to another, the basic construction of letters remains the same, as does the connective process of assembling those letters. The forger is not going to be able to reproduce all of that either quickly or without a great deal of effort. So the first thing to look for in a suspected forgery is clues to the writing speed. If there are shaky curves, heavy pressure, blunt finishing strokes and deliberate instead of free-flowing loops or flourishes, these all point to slow speed.

Some of the finer points of a writing style that a forger will probably miss, and which are worth checking:

(a) *Word spacing.* A difficult habit to break if the forger's natural spacing differs from the victim's; use a ruler to measure spacing carefully.

(b) *Slant.* This is usually consistent for most writers, but it is difficult for a forger to maintain.

(c) *Word endings.* Producing each word is tiring for the forger, who tends to relax towards the end of a word, making mistakes in the last letter and end stroke.

(d) *i-dots and t-bars.* Although we tend to vary our style in writing these (the i-dots especially), it is likely that the forger will be more deliberate in dot placement (consistently over the i) and bar length.

(e) *Breaks in words, where the pen has been lifted and replaced.* The forger will tend to produce more of these.

(f) *Slope of the line of writing.* The forger will probably not produce a rising or falling line.

(g) *Sizes of capitals and lengths of upper and lower loops.* Although the forger may imitate these well, they will probably end up larger than they should.

(h) *All middle zone letter shapes, slants and connections.* A letter-by-letter comparison should reveal a lot of small discrepancies.

(i) *Pressure.* The forgery is likely to have heavier and less even pressure.

(j) *Size variation.* The forgery is likely to be slightly different in size from the original.

There are more than enough factors here for you to identify any piece of forged writing as such. Unless the forgery is staggeringly well accomplished, forgery detection is a very easy job for the graphologist. Similarly, it is difficult for a person to conceal their natural style of handwriting; a letter-by-letter comparison similar to that suggested in the ten points above, but looking for similarities rather than discrepancies, should reveal the truth.

A forgery exposed

ANALYSIS: number 2 of the four is a poor forgery attempt because:

(a) The start of the other three is slightly leftward, while the forgery is upright and slightly rightward.

(b) Smoothness is lacking in most strokes of the forgery – note especially the p loops and the g loop.

(c) The Greek E initial is narrower with a larger centre in the forgery.

(d) The t-bar goes to a point in the other three.

(e) Both examples of the letter u have sharks' teeth in the three genuine signatures but are more rounded in the forgery.

(f) The forgery's spacing is wrong – too much between the E and the D.

(g) The u begins at its highest point except in the forgery.

(h) The forgery had invisible joins where the pen was lifted and replaced, especially n-e and a-t.

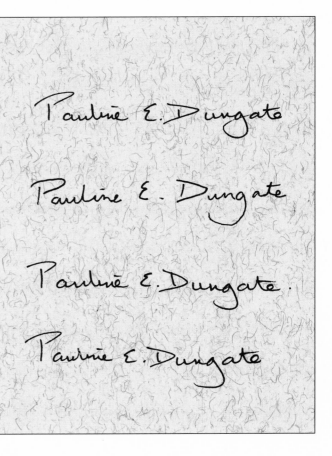

Vocational guidance

Graphology is an excellent method of helping a person find the right career. However, in the case of children or teenagers there may be problems due to the fact that their handwriting is still immature. Analysing writing correctly and recommending the most suitable areas of work is a job for the professional graphologist, not something that can be done for oneself or learnt from a beginner's book.

On the other hand, there are many adults who feel frustrated because their jobs or careers are inappropriate for them. While graphology will not tell you exactly what job you should be doing (despite the claims of some books), it can help you to discover what basic type of employment would be suitable for somebody with your personality.

This is not the same as applying for a job and either being accepted or rejected according to an analysis of your handwriting. Once you have established the type of job that would suit you best, you can start applying or retraining for that sort of thing. Most organizations require a huge range of different types of people to perform different functions, so it might be that a move to a different position within the same organization would reveal a hitherto dormant talent and help to make you feel less frustrated.

Because of the wide range of job types and the mix of qualities required for each, only a few examples can be given here. You are likely to be suitable for a job in a particular area if your handwriting satisfies at least half the listed points.

The artistic job

Art, design, architecture.

Wide word and letter spacing, wide left-hand margin, i-dot meticulously placed or in the form of a circle, punctuation carefully inserted, disconnected letters or arcade connections, perhaps a lengthy t-bar to the right, perhaps pastose writing, wide letters, perhaps smallish non-uniform letters, perhaps tall and simple capitals, perhaps upright writing.

The routine business job

Office work, typing, clerical work, VDU operation.

Wide spacing, perhaps t-bar thick and joining the next letter, lack of starting strokes, i-dot carefully placed, punctuation careful, small writing, garland or angular connections, right slant, simplified style, no lower zone loops, legible writing, g and y resemble 8 and 7, regular writing with a heavy but fairly even pressure, knotted f, k and t.

The management job

In charge of other workers in any sort of office-based organization.

Smallish printed capitals, a and o left slightly open, t-bar thick and joining the next letter, wide spacing, perhaps careful punctuation, perhaps no starting strokes, regular writing, i-dot carefully placed, t-bar as a strong convex curve across the stem, g like an 8, m and n like w and u, upward slope, right slant, fast writing, wide spacing, no lower zone loops, large middle zone, large and even word spacing, perhaps angular connection, upper and lower zones of the f well balanced, heavy pressure.

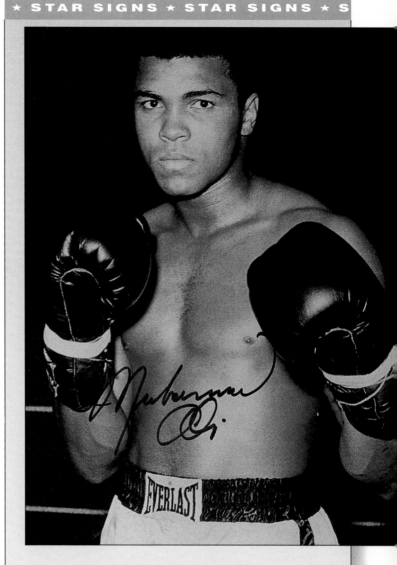

Muhammad Ali

This is the name and signature adopted by Cassius Clay when he became a Muslim in his twenties. Its careful balance looks artificial. The large size would have come naturally to the showman within Ali; the large capitals and oversize l-loop have similar origins.

The way in which the M extends below the baseline indicates strength and vigour. The d, with its open curve to the left, is typical of those with a determination to succeed, but it also carries connotations of his literary talent (remember "I float like a butterfly, sting like a bee" and similar poetic endeavours).

An interesting point is why the signature is across the solar plexus rather than the white of the shorts, where it would show up much better. The answer is probably that Ali was indicating great pride in his black skin and his superior physique by drawing attention to them.

The selling job

Commercial traveller, sales representative.

Printed capitals, open a and o, t-bar heavy and joining next letter or long and rising, wide spacing, fast and simplified style, f loops balanced (similar length in the upper and lower zones), letters h and m and n form v shapes, i-dot to the right as a dash, a larger than normal capital I (personal pronoun), right slant, maybe long initial strokes, angular connections, upward slope, upper zone larger than lower, large writing, heavy pressure, a rising and perhaps underlined signature.

S ★ STAR SIGNS ★ STAR SIGNS ★

Isaac Asimov

Here it is the ornate double and treble loops inside the letters a, c, o and s that catch the eye. They are meant to signify untruthfulness, which is perhaps no bad thing if you are the best-known science-fiction writer in the world!

The large signature suggests self-importance or forcefulness, with a touch of the show-off in those capitals. This is obviously an optimistic signature from a fluent, fast-thinking person who is alert, adaptable and spontaneous, with lots of enthusiasm.

Surprisingly, there are no real signs of Asimov the workaholic, who wrote more than 400 books and was never happy when away from his typewriter.

The scientific job

Research, testing, fieldwork, teaching.

g and y like 8 and 7, i-dot carefully placed close to stem, no starting strokes, wide spacing, careful punctuation, simplified style, right slant or upright, small writing,

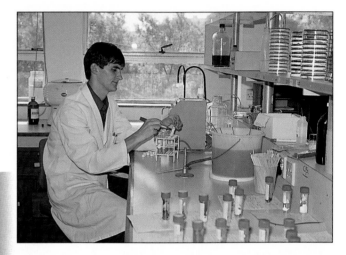

angular connections, narrow letters, t-bar bisected by stem, no lower zone loops, legible, quick writing, heavy pressure, perhaps knots in f, k and t, a and o closed, sometimes writes all in neat printed capitals.

The job with people

Counselling, law, nursing, social work.

Printed capitals, perhaps wide spacing, g like an 8, m and n like w and u, right slant, t-stroke covers whole word or is wavy, g and y endings to the right, narrowing words, perhaps arcade connections, perhaps disconnected, round letters, upward slope, i-dot as a dash to the right, perhaps upper zone more noticeable, m and n with rounded tops, light pressure, easy flow, wide letters, last letter smaller, perhaps closed a and o.

The practical job

A craft or trade.

Wide left margin, good spacing, perhaps a circled i-dot, exact dotting of i, careful punctuation, long swinging loops, pressure firm and even, perhaps small writing, perhaps angular, perhaps narrow and simplified writing, perhaps printed capitals, strong convex t-bar through stem, no breaks or amendments, steady line, end of e turns down, lower-case letters closed.

Choosing a compatible partner

Not only is this a very tricky area, since one person's ideal lifetime partner is another person's worst possible choice, but nobody is really going to marry somebody else on the basis of a sample of their handwriting. On the other hand, there are certain negative traits that can be identified from handwriting which will make that person very tough to live with, while there are certain positive traits which generally bode well.

So here are two lists of handwriting characteristics.

The first lists handwriting characteristics of people with whom it is better to avoid having long-term relationships. They may be aggressive, or bullies, or deceitful, or demand their own way all the time, or simply be totally stubborn. They may never be more than two seconds from an hysterical outburst, or they may never show emotion at all, or they may go in for sexual teasing, or pessimism, or be obsessed with their own appearance or their work, or be regularly forgetful. If you are already married to somebody with one or more of these flaws, you will appreciate the problem. Of course, people are complex and contradictory, and certain negative character traits will be balanced by positive features. This will be reflected in the handwriting. Look, therefore, for particular trends and patterns in the style which predominate.

AVOID relationships with people whose writing is like this

- very right or left slanted
- changes of slant in the same sample
- descending lines or letters within a word
- completely illegible
- equal margins
- very straight lines
- extremely even spacing
- letters clogged with ink
- strong diagonal starting stroke for any letter
- hooks on capitals
- a small circle at the start of any letter
- a relatively large middle zone
- double loop on letters a, c, g, o
- d or t forming a tent-shape at the base
- d or t ending thickly below the base line
- d, e or t with a thick horizontal ending
- d stem slanting more to the right than other letters
- d stem much taller than the middle zone
- d with the stem detached from the circular part
- d or t with a talon shape beneath it
- g and y with a rightward stem
- g with a very long stem
- g or y with a triangular loop
- g or y with a thickening stem (going down)
- g or y with a sharp angle in its stem
- g or y with a blunt end or needle end to its stem
- g or y with a sharp upward angle at the stem end
- g with a plain, straight stem
- h and n sharply angled at top and bottom
- i-dot carefully placed and directly above the stem
- i-dots missing
- I much larger than the middle zone
- K or R with arms piercing the stem
- sharp peaks on m (upper- and lower-case)
- M beginning with a sharp peak higher than the rest
- sharks' teeth in m or n
- o with a line in the middle
- t-bar evenly across stem
- t-bar detached to the right
- t-bar missing
- t-bar above stem
- t-bar as a star
- t-bar sloping down to the right and thicker at end
- t-bar like a needle
- descending signature
- signature with large, embellished capitals

zany doings

Letters clogged with ink

African police

Double loop on a, c, g and o

secosch

d with detached stem

t my his

g or y with sharp angle

coast

t-bar as a star

nomal

Small circle at start

the

ard n

d or t in tent shape

ying

g or y with triangular stem

kird

k or r with arms piercing stem

On the other hand, there are many positive characteristics to be found. The second list indicates handwriting characteristics of people who make good partners. They tend to be faithful, or considerate, or understandingly sensitive, or friendly, or optimistic, always saying the right thing at the right time. Or they may be quick-thinking, may have a good sense of humour, may enjoy the good life, may have plenty of flexibility and common sense. They tend not to let themselves get bogged down in tradition or red tape, but may be imaginative, highly sensual and with plenty of sexual energy. Be warned – you will be unlikely to find all these qualities in a single person.

GO FOR relationships with people whose writing is like this:
- slight right slant
- use of a broad pen
- rising lines
- any mistakes heavily crossed out
- heavy writing
- any word diminishing in size
- any upper- or lower-case letter with a wavy line in it or connecting it
- any letter with a smile line in it
- any wavy paraph
- any paraph resembling a smile line
- a and o very round
- a and o clear inside
- d stem without a loop, curving up to the left
- d or t with a short stem
- d or t with a looped stem
- d, e, h, m, n or t with a cup-hook curved ending stroke or a high-rising ending stroke
- upper- or lower-case Greek e
- f with equal loops at top and bottom
- g like an s or an 8
- g with a very full loop
- g or y resembling q
- i-dot small and round
- upper-case K with arms that loop stem
- upper- or lower-case m resembling undotted i in parallel
- r with two peaks
- t-bar serving two or more ts
- t-bar rising
- t-bar very long
- rising signature
- rising signature with a single rising paraph

Thursday

Smile lines

_be_

Greek e

money

Shark's teeth

differ markedly

Left-curving d stem, no loop

grating

g like s or an 8

Twenties

t-bar long and/or rising

71

Signs of illness

The two most important signs of infirmity, caused by age and illness, are shaky writing that doesn't flow (above) and spaces or pauses within words (below).

A number of graphologists have carried out research which points to there being unmistakable clues of illness in one's handwriting. All these seem to be unconscious changes from the person's previously healthy state of writing. Some of the evidence seems miraculous and hard to account for.

Certain signs of depression and tiredness have already been mentioned (especially descending lines, small writing, weak pressure and a missing t-bar). Emotional disturbances may produce great fluctuations in the size of letters, or irregular spacing of words, or variable pressure, or perhaps concealed middle zone letters or downstrokes that are not parallel.

Any physically debilitating illness can result in smaller than usual writing and weak pressure (or perhaps very heavy pressure). In more serious cases the general form level of the writing will deteriorate, speed will decrease, strokes will lose fluency and become shaky, frequent breaks or pauses will become apparent, and touch-up strokes or amendments will occur (or occur more frequently). Some of these handwriting symptoms may be noticeable before physical symptoms of the illness have been realized.

In addition, some handwriting traits that are commonly blamed on ego problems may be the result of illness. For example, very tiny handwriting is explicable not only in terms of a small ego or a lack of self-confidence or depression but by short-sightedness. And large handwriting, while it may show a big ego, may also be a cover for loss of motor control (as in Parkinson's disease) because it is easier to write large in a neat hand.

In cases of mental illness the person's normal handwriting becomes distorted. Sudden changes in the signature, including down-sloping or ornamentation or crossing out, are significant here. But such changes are unlikely to be isolated. There may be a shrinking of the middle zone, or an abandonment of normal word spacing, or frequent underlining, or an extreme slant so that the writing is almost lying down (to the left or the right).

In *The Secret Self* (London, 1988) graphologist Anna Koren describes how a person who has lost a leg will truncate a lower zone loop unconsciously after his or her loss. If it is the left leg the truncation occurs at the beginning of a word, and if it is the right leg, at the end of a word.

Even more surprising (and much more useful) it seems that the writer who is physically ill will pause momentarily in his or her writing in an appropriate place. The pauses will correspond to affected parts of the body in this way: upper zone loops of lower-case letters if the illness affects the head or face; middle zone letters if it is a problem of the chest or abdomen; lower zone loops if the legs or feet are the seat of the problem. What this tiny unconscious pause will do is to produce a small dot, usually invisible to the naked eye but visible through a magnifying glass. Koren, who has researched such dots, even relates an anecdote about disovering pregnancy this way – only two days after conception.

Other graphologists, too, have noticed peculiarities creeping into a zone which corresponds to an area of the body when illness appears. Apparently, migraines can show themselves in the upper zone as slightly bent stems of such letters as b, d, h and t. Stomach problems can manifest themselves as lighter pressure in the middle zone. Some distortion of the lower zone, or even a small gap in a downstroke there, is an indicator of leg pain.

Obviously, this is a fascinating and still developing area of graphological analysis.

Adolf Hitler

Even at a time when his power was increasing and he should have been optimistic about the future (1938), Hitler persisted with this abnormally angled signature, which strongly indicates depression and pessimism. The large gap between initial and surname could mean shyness and introversion, yet the signature seems to be excessively right-slanted, suggesting a strongly extrovert, even megalomaniac, personality; the extreme formality of the single initial in fact adds weight to the first impression.

The lack of i-dots and t-bars can mean either rebelliousness or resourcefulness. Some egotism is suggested by the two heavy downstrokes (the mis-angled cross-strokes of the A and H). While this is almost illegible as a signature, it must have been well known to most, if not all, Germans of the period as a kind of cypher. Its strangeness may therefore be regarded as a mark of vanity in itself. Angular connections were very common in the older German Gothic script, so this factor may be ignored.

Change your writing style and change your personality?

If you have read this far through the book, it is probable that you will have discovered several aspects of your own handwriting which suggest personality defects. Maybe your writing is illegible. Perhaps it tends to be very small and to descend towards the end of the line. Maybe there are hooks or small loops all over your letters. Or it could be that you write in a highly ornate and embellished style.

You may be asking, "What can I do about it?"

The first thing to be said is that almost everybody's handwriting has one or two rather negative elements, so don't worry.

But if you really do not want anybody else to know that you are inconsiderate with perhaps something to hide (illegible handwriting) or depressed (very small and descending), jealous (hooks and small loops) or a vain and pompous show-off (embellishments), then you can do something about your writing style.

Certainly it is possible to identify these elements in your writing and, with practice, to cultivate an alternative style of writing which eliminates them. Nobody is suggesting that you should change your handwriting completely; usually it is enough to work on just a few elements. It must be said that to effect any permanent change to your handwriting will require a considerable amount of hard work. You have probably been writing as you do for a decade or two, so it could easily take months of daily practice to replace a negative element with a positive one.

Why should you bother? Very few people will look at your writing and recognize the personality defect (though it may be evident to them from your behaviour). Unfortunately, one of those few people to see your writing could be a graphologist, especially if you are applying for a job with a different firm or hoping to get promotion with your present employer. So it could be well worth while ridding your writing of all those signs of unreliability and dishonesty.

If you do change your handwriting, you may wonder whether it will make any difference to your personality? Or will all the defects remain, but just be hidden from the graphologist?

The answer is not that simple. Like any other self-help approach, half the battle is in identifying and accepting the problem. If you are willing to accept that the verdict of generations of graphologists is that your writing shows certain personality defects, and if you are determined to correct them, then the chances are that you will succeed. Of course, changing a few aspects of your handwriting is not going to make any difference to a major emotional or psychological problem that needs to be treated by a doctor, but many more minor problems can be helped.

Let us return to the initial examples and see both how a change of style could be managed and what that change might do to help you.

Illegibility (as mentioned in Chapter 8) is almost always due to trying too write to fast. If this is your problem you must learn to curb your impatience and write more slowly. That is rather more easily said than done. A radical solution might be to study calligraphy, since if you can learn to write good, even, ornate letters at a snail's pace it will help you to achieve the patience and degree of exactness you need to write legibly on a regular basis. Alternatively, concentrate on managing more exactness (and therefore legibility) in some areas of your writing. For example, practice dotting each i and crossing each t in a regular and controlled manner – a

Sean Connery

As with many well-known figures, Sean Connery assumes that his signature will be recognized and thus does not worry about making it legible. The most noticeable feature is the bulk of the surname, resembling a letter i in series; this suggests intuition and versatility.

There is a surprising lack of showmanship here, with a signature of modest size, lacking flourishes or paraphs. These traits, together with the lack of slant, reveal a well-balanced person without hang-ups or ego problems. His almost fully joined letters mark him out as a logical thinker who plans ahead.

Only the missing o of Connery (haste, lack of care), the treble loop in the a of Sean (suggesting a person who is not always honest) and the sharp tail of the concluding y (a sharp mind, but a stubborn one) give an inkling of anything amiss.

coming *coming*

With a thick point it's easy to be illegible.

With a finer point it's less easy.

Cramming your letters and words together makes for difficult reading.

Broader spacing helps legibility.

I'm going to be happy

I'm going to be happy

I'm going to be happy

I'm going to be happy

I'm going to be happy

Four ways in which you can work to improve poor handwriting, from top to bottom: taking care over second half of words; writing with a finer penpoint; developing a broader style that extends further across the page; practising positive sentences with a final flourish.

small round dot directly above and close to the i stem, and a straight level bar bisected by the t stem. You could also try to concentrate more on the second half of each word (which is where the impatient scribble is usually at its worst), and you could switch to a finer point on your pen (so that each stroke is more easily differentiated from others). If the illegibility is due to narrow letter, word or line spacing you should try to widen all of these. The end result could be a more careful and painstaking personality, in your handwriting and in your life.

If you are seriously depressed you should seek medical help. Where the condition is slight or occasional you will need to improve your self-image. In non-writing ways this can include finding new interests, meeting new people, changing your physical image with new clothes and concentrating your mind on the areas of life where you are successful. In writing ways it means learning to put a bit of exuberance into your words. You could begin with your signature. Try writing it larger than normal and sloping upwards. Make it stand out by adding a single straight line (or a smile line) beneath it. Practise this for five or ten minutes each day, getting a rhythm going. Also, find a short sentence that ends with a y (recommended is "I'm going to be happy") and write it repeatedly for five or ten minutes a day. Make sure you end the sentence with a flourish that takes the tail out of the y curving round and far up to the right, higher than any of the other letters. Another exercise is to practise spreading out your letters so that your middle zone vowels become broad. Make sure that they are circular and clear inside.

The hooks and loops of a writing style can be overcome by simplification. Try to begin with an unadorned downstroke. Switch over to printed capitals if necessary. This will not necessarily do anything for a jealous nature, for which the best treatment is probably reassurance by your partner (who should be involved in any of these attempts at change).

Embellishment of any sort can be cut out or toned down by switching over to the simplest of printed capitals. Because your writing is probably very slow (it is difficult to be ornate or to add embellishment at anything other than a slow and deliberate pace) the simplification will almost certainly enable you to write faster, which will help to prevent any curlicues slipping in again. Most ornate writers (though not all) are rather infrequent writers, so it might help you to take on a regular writing commitment: try keeping a diary and buy yourself a large one (preferably one A4 page per day).

It would be simplistic to believe that changing any feature of your handwriting is easy or that miraculous personality changes will result. But remember that change is possible. Your handwriting will always reflect the kind of person you are, and by learning to write in a different style you may well be able to improve a personality defect.

This chapter has dealt with only four examples out of many possibilities. Almost all other handwriting defects are susceptible to change if you are determined enough. Analyse your writing and design your own exercises for improvement.

★ STAR SIGNS ★ STAR SIGNS ★ S

Henry Ford

Pride, self-importance and even vanity can be deduced from the very large signature. The large middle zone is one of the marks of leadership. There is also ambition evident in the width of the letters.

This is a very slowly written and tightly controlled signature, indicating a precise, unemotional planner. The simplicity of the letters, making them very easily understood, is an attention-grabbing ruse by somebody who is determined to be known. The slowness also indicates a methodical and thorough person. Only the terminal stroke of the d, dipping below the base line, adds a negative aspect, with its connotations of reticence, selfishness and intolerance.

Index

Picture credits

British Film Institute: 73. J. Allan Cash Ltd: 64, 65 (left), 66 (right). Jill-Anne de Cet: 71, 75. The Joel Finler Collection: 40, 46. Sally and Richard Greenhill: 9. Chris Morgan: 66 (left). NASA: 20. Richard Nixon Library and Birthplace, Yorba Linda, CA: 22. Pictorial Press: 31, 58, 61. Popperfoto: 8. Naomi Stadlen: 10. Wide World Photos: 7.

Steve Gilbert of Signpost supplied the autographs on pages 33, 58, 61, 65 and 66.